M000006802

FINNISH TOUCHES

RECIPES & TRADITIONS

Fantastically Finnish
revised and expanded

"Swans" by sculptor Armas Hurti, Helsinki, Finland
Immigrants' Monument, Thunder Bay, Ontario, Canada

Penfield
BOOKS

ACKNOWLEDGMENTS

We thank those who have contributed to either *Finnish Touches: Recipes and Traditions* or to *Fantastically Finnish*, first published in 1982. America's noted Scandinavian recipe authority, Beatrice Ojakangas of Duluth, Minnesota, served as food and recipe editor of *Fantastically Finnish*. Her essays and many of the recipes she selected are included in this book. In addition to those listed in the book, we especially thank Jim Kurtti, editor; David Maki, assistant editor of the *Finnish American Reporter*, Hancock, Michigan; Brenda Warren of Concordia Language Villages; Helena Niskanen of the Finnish Tourist Board; and Marja Guercin of the Embassy of Finland, Washington, D.C.

Editors: Joan Liffring-Zug Bourret, Gerry Kangas, and Dorothy Crum
Associate Editors: Maureen Patterson, Melinda Bradnan, Dwayne Bourret, and Liz Rolfsmeier
Illustrations: Diane Heusinkveld
Graphics: Deborah Walkoczy Croes
Front cover photograph and photo at right by Joan Liffring-Zug Bourret

Front Cover:
Väkkärä, the award-winning folk music group shown on the front cover, is named after a traditional toy of Ähtäri, Finland, the city in which the group was founded in 1993, and where the fifteen-member group continues to reside. Performing at Toronto in 2000 were: (center) Tiina Savola with accordion, (left to right) Ilkka Knuuttila, Mikko Savola, Heikki Savola, Anne-Mari Isoaho, Riikka Lamminaho, Jenni Seppälä.

Finland State Forest, Finland, Minnesota

ISBN 0-9717-025-2-7   LCCN 2002104646   Copyright 2002 Penfield Books

2–

DEDICATED
to all who have *sisu*

Lydia Torry, 1950s

Finlandia University at Hancock, Michigan, defines *sisu* as "persistence and determination." There are many varieties of *sisu*. *Sisu* can be a sudden outburst or it can be the kind that lasts. It is strength and endurance beyond reason. It is in the soul, coming from within itself.

Lydia Torry, who lived alone for many years on a remote island in Lake Namakan in Minnesota, was a remarkable example of *sisu*. Her neighbors were the deer, bears, and the birds. Over forty years ago, my family, with our two young sons, stopped to see her each summer. Lydia greeted hundreds of visitors every summer, showing her home, sauna, and other buildings accessible only by boat in the summer. If she needed help, she stamped S.O.S. in the snow. A native of Finland, Mrs. Torry lost her husband Emil, a commercial fisherman, but stayed on the island until her health forced a change. She always planted flowers and a large vegetable garden, including carrots in an abandoned little boat. Today, her island is a part of Voyageur National Park.

—Joan Liffring-Zug Bourret

SCENES IN FINLAND

by Gerry Kangas

The traditional bonfire is a familiar scene along Finland's lakeshores at midsummer festival time. This is when Finns celebrate the longest day of the year, the Finnish flag, and always on June 24, St. John the Baptist's feast day. Bright fields of yellow mustard surround the stone ramparts of Suomenlinna, the fortress of Finland in Helsinki. The fortress, built for the Swedish empire in 1748, is now a favorite picnic spot.

CONTENTS

IMPORTANT DATES IN FINNISH HISTORY

8000–6000 B.C.: Approximate time of first humans in Finland after the Ice Age. Relics show production of fish nets.

500 B.C.–A.D. 500: Arrival of Finno-Ugrian peoples, possibly from the Ural Mountains—a conclusion based on language similarities of present-day peoples.

12th Century: King Eric of Sweden and Bishop Henry of Upsala brought Christianity to Finland. Turku became the ecclesiastical headquarters.

1293: Castle of Wiborg was built by Swedish forces as an "Eastland" outpost against attacks from the east. The war-and-peace eras between Sweden and Russia were already under way.

1397–1523: The Kalmar Union united the Scandinavian monarchies of Denmark, Sweden, and Norway politically for the only time in history. United under the Danish crown, antagonisms developed with the Swedish nobility, which controlled both Sweden and Finland, causing the union to fail. Finland suffered as a result of the turmoil. Gustavus I Vasa became king of Sweden and founded the dynasty that ruled Sweden-Finland for more than a century. Reign of Gustavus Vasa led the Reformation, and in 1544, declared the monarchy hereditary. His reign led to the beginnings of the Lutheran Church.

1638: Finns came with the Swedes to Wilmington, Delaware.

1640: Åbo Academy of Turku founded. It was later moved to Helsinki, becoming the University of Helsinki, the center of higher education in Finland.

1618–48: The Thirty Years' War. Finns fought as members of the Swedish forces.

1710: Armies of Peter the Great, Czar of Russia, conquered Finland. Russian occupation ended in 1721. Sweden resumed control of Finland.

1741–43: Russia again overran Finland, withdrawing under the 1743 Treaty of Turku.

1776: First newspaper in Finnish, *Tieto-Sanomat,* was published.

1807–09: Russia again retook Finland, which became a Grand Duchy of Russia with considerable autonomy. Helsinki, destroyed in the war, was rebuilt.

1812: Helsinki became the capital of Finland.

1828: University moved to Helsinki after a severe fire in Turku.

1835: The *Kalevala,* the Finnish epic by Elias Lönnrot, was published, giving rise to the importance of literature in fostering national consciousness.

1863: Finnish became an official administrative language.

1864–1920: Approximately 300,000 Finns set sail for America. Many settled in Michigan and Minnesota.

1878: The Conscription Act gave Finland an army of its own.

1906: Finland was the first European country giving women the right to vote.

1917: Russian government was overthrown; Finland declared its independence on December 6.

1918: Civil War between "Red" militia in the south and "White" government security forces, led by Gustaf Emil Mannerheim.

1919: On July 17, the parliament adopted a constitution.

1920s: Finland won many friends in the United States by making annual payments on debts contracted after it became independent.

1921–22: The League of Nations granted the disputed claim between Sweden and Finland of the strategic Åland Islands to Finland. The Language Act of 1922 declared both Finnish and Swedish to be official languages.

1939: The Soviet Union proposed to cede lands that would move the Finnish border eastward in exchange for certain islands in the Gulf of Finland, Hanko Peninsula, and southern Karelia. Finland refused, and shortly was attacked by Russia in the bitter three-month Winter War, which ended March 13, 1940, with Finland ceding territories to Russia.

1941–44: The "Second Phase" of the war. Finns retake the land ceded to the Soviet Union by the terms of the Winter War, but are forced to return it under terms of another peace accord, which sets a date by which all German troops must be out of Finland.

1944–45: The Lapland War, led by Finnish General Hjalmar Siilasvuo against German troops in northern Finland, devastated large areas. The Karelians chose to live in Finland, most of them walking out of their native land—now Russian—with only what they could carry. They were welcomed by the Finns.

1950s–60s: Economic changes after World War II caused the Great Migration within Finland. Population shifted from rural areas to the urban, industrialized south. Mechanization of agriculture and forestry eliminated jobs, and an aging population began to abandon farms. This trend saw the establishment of two of Helsinki's suburbs: Espoo in 1963 and Vantaa in 1972, which grew to be the country's fourth and fifth largest cities.

1952: The Olympic Games were held in Helsinki.

1955: The Soviet Union withdrew from Porkkala and returned the area to Finland. Finland joined the United Nations and Nordic Council.

1972–1975: The Council for Equality was established to advise lawmakers on realizing full legal equality for women. The Helsinki Accords formed an important basis for human rights.

1980s–90s: Economic development with inflation created devaluations in currency and a cycle of erosion of "boom" economy. Cultural and social life were influenced by student radicalism and the other phenomenon, the Finnish version of rock-and-roll, *"Suomirokki."* The collapse of the Soviet Union and the end of Cold War turned a new page in the history of Finland.

2000–present: Current Finland is a peace-loving, democratic country, having made a long journey from isolated and rugged hunters to a cultivated high-tech nation. It has twenty universities and colleges of higher education, all open to foreign students as well as Finns.

FINLAND TODAY

Midnight sun, modern architecture, saunas, and reindeer are among the symbols of Finland. The sixth-largest European country, bordered on the west by Sweden, on the north by Norway, and on the east by Russia, Finland has 305,470 square kilometers of land and 31,560 square kilometers of inland water. The force of moving ice sheets from the continental glaciers influenced the shaping of the country's surface—leaving behind thousands of lakes.

In 2000, Finland elected its first woman president, Tarja Halonen.

Finland's rugged coastline; south on the Gulf of Finland, southwest on the Baltic Sea, and west on the Gulf of Bothnia; is carved with bays and inlets. Extending from the southwestern coast into the Baltic Sea, archipelago Finland consists of thousands of forest-covered and bedrock islands and skerries, which continue to be formed, even now, more than a hundred centuries after the recession of the continental glaciers. Scientific studies indicate that land continues to emerge from the sea, adding to the country's land mass.

Clay plains along the coast support agriculture. The interior lake district, the largest geographic region, provides extensive forests. In the extreme north of Upland Finland, extending beyond the Arctic Circle, is Lapland, covered with Arctic scrub, while the southernmost region of the country is essentially bogland. Each of the areas, however, has elements of the other; patches of agriculture are seen far northward.

Some traditional folk theories suggest that Finnic tribes may have begun to establish themselves in present-day Finland as early as 3000 B.C. Among those tribes who eventually merged with one another are the Suomalaiset, who migrated to southwestern Finland and inland, and from whom the name Suomi (Finland) was derived; the Tavastians migrated inland in the south; Karelians settled farther east in the present-day Karelian

Isthmus and Lake Ladoga area; the Estonians lived on the southern coast of the Gulf of Finland. In the far north were the Lapps (Sami), who even though speaking a Finno-Ugric language, did not assimilate with the indigenous population.

Finland became virtually free of minority and religious divisions. The Swedish-speaking Finns, the largest minority group, dropped from 12 percent to 6 percent of the population in the twentieth century. The Lapps and the Gypsies still remain a very small minority. Even though Finns belong to a few dozen churches, the Lutheran Church of Finland has nearly 90 percent of the population as members, and the Orthodox Church of Finland is next in size with a much smaller membership.

Since World War II, Finland has become one of the most advanced societies in the world. Its population of around 5 million-plus citizens is guaranteed a decent quality of life through protective legislative measures.

The forests of Finland are still important for the production of high-quality papers and other related products, but electronic technology has become a major industry; machinery and metal production account for a large percentage of the economy, with the remainder mostly chemical and clothing products.

Finland has a long tradition in shipbuilding. One of the most unique is the Finnish icebreaker, which keeps sea channels open year-round. The Kvaerner Masa Yards in Helsinki and Turku produce many of the world's cruise liners as well as special vessels using the latest technical and ergonomic principles.

Warmed by the Gulf Stream, Finland has four distinct seasons. In the summertime, the sun shines fifteen hours a day; in the far north, it is light enough to read outdoors at midnight! Sometime between October and April, the "Northern Lights" appear to brighten the darkened winter sky.

The largest cities in order of size, after Helsinki, are Espoo, Tampere, Vantaa, Turku, Oulu, Lahti, Kuopio, Pori, and Jyväskylä.

Helsinki, the capital city of over half a million people, was recognized as one of the European Cities of Culture in the year 2000. Overlooking the Gulf of Finland and the coastal archipelago, Helsinki became the capital city of the Grand Duchy of Finland in 1812. Following the 1917 independence of Finland, the city grew to reflect the trends of the new republic. Overcoming the devastation of World War II, Helsinki hosted the 1952 Summer Olympics, which strengthened its reputation as an international metropolis.

The capital city is a blend of the past and present, nature and metropolis. The impressive architecture, tree-lined streets, colorful markets, and waterfront are due in part to the efforts of such modernist Finnish designers as Alvar Aalto. The Temppeliaukiokirkko (Rock Church) is an example of the mix of nature and architecture. Senate Square is a further "living work of art" with the majestic Lutheran cathedral, the Council of State building, and the main building of the University of Helsinki. Nationally Finland displays a wealth of talent and international influence in the fields of architectural and product design, the visual arts, literature, and music.

In Helsinki, sixty museums and galleries display international arts, lifestyle, and historical exhibits. Most prominent among these are the Helsinki City Museum, the Ateneum, and Kiasma, the Museum of Contemporary Art. The unique styles of Finnish architecture are highlights of the National Museum of Finland and the Museum of Finnish Architecture. Other notable sites include the Lasipalatsi (Glass Palace) Film and Media Center and the Tennispalatsi (Tennis Palace), originally built for the Olympics, now a cultural and leisure center. The Winter Garden blossoms year round; Finlandia Hall and the spectacular Opera House are centers of the music world; the Sibelius monument in Sibelius Park is stunning in design and monumental size.

Distinctive Finnish products may be observed in the Arabia Ceramic Factory; at glass-blowing plants in Nuutajärvi, Riihimäki, and Iittala; in textile design by Finlayson Sisustustekstiili Oy, Marimekko Oy, and Woodnotes Oy; and at Design Forum Finland, maintained by the Finnish Society of Crafts and Design.

The Helsinki Herring (*Strömming*) Fair, happening the first week in October each year, has a history dating back to 1545. Along with the traditional salted and pickled herring, other fish and exotic condiments are available, as well as socks, hats, pullovers, and other apparel made by the islanders from the wool of sheep on the remote islands. Loaves of delicious black archipelago bread are also featured.

Nearby on the islands is Suomenlinna, the "Gibraltar of the North," a former fortress. Korkeasaari Island houses one of the northernmost zoos in the world; the Seurasaari Open-Air Museum features architecture and lifestyle exhibits from various regions, including the wooden Karuna Church, completed in 1686.

History and nature come alive in the areas surrounding Helsinki. In Uusimaa, the "Capital County," stretching east and west of Helsinki, there are quaint settlements, medieval villages, and historic manors. To the west is Espoo, with a history dating back 8,000 years; further west, Tammisaari features seventeenth- and eighteenth-century wooden architecture; the capetown of Hanko has an annual regatta in July.

Turku, Finland's oldest city and the country's former capital, boasts a thirteenth-century castle, medieval cathedral, and other historically significant buildings along with a Handicrafts Museum, Aboa Vetus (old Turku), Ars Nova (contemporary art) museum, and the new Forum Marinum. Nearby in the town of Naantali is one of Finland's finest spas; the Naantali Chamber Music Festival in June is internationally acclaimed. Close by, cartoons come to life at Moominworld. Further north, in Rauma, third-oldest town in Finland and a UNESCO World Heritage Site, the extraordinary lace-making industry can be observed. Eura, east of Rauma, exhibits archeological finds from the Viking Era; at Sammallahdenmäki, also a UNESCO World Heritage Site, are thirty-three burial cairns of the Bronze Age.

East of Helsinki is Porvoo, Finland's second-oldest town dating back to 1346. Further eastward is Loviisa, a frontier and fortress town dating back to 1745. Farther eastward, on the archipelago of Kotka, is the St. Nicholas Orthodox Church, constructed in 1799; next to Kotka is the unique star-shaped fortress town of Hamina.

The Finnish Lakeland region is one of Europe's largest inland waterway systems. During the summer, cruises interconnect lakeside towns and notable sites; some offer coach tours. Within easy reach from Helsinki in the Western Lake District is the city of Tampere, where high tech and culture flourish side by side with historic sites, art exhibits, and museums. The Särkänniemi complex houses a dolphinarium, aquarium, planetarium, and observation tower. Flanked by 200 unspoiled lakes and the Tammerkoski Rapids that run through the city, Tampere Hall is the largest concert hall in Scandinavia and the center of international festivals including: a Film Festival in March, Vocal Music Festival in June, International

Theatre Festival in August, and the Tampere Jazz Happening in November.

The Alvar Aalto Museum, a tribute to Finland's famous architect, is located in the Central Lakeland region, as is the Regional Museum of Central Finland. In Eastern Finland, the town of Savonlinna spreads over a chain of islands, and is the site of the world-famous Savonlinna Opera Festival, attracting thousands of people each year.

Photograph by Gerry Kangas

Wooden Orthodox chapel in Nurmes, Finland

National Nature Symbols

"Nature symbols," to draw attention to Finland's natural beauty and wildlife, were chosen by popular vote during the 1980s–'90s. They represent traditional significance going back to ancient times.

Lily of the Valley

In the first vote for a national flower, most rural Finns favored the cornflower or ox-eye daisy since the lily of the valley was known as a medicinal plant and essentially poisonous. With an increasingly urban culture it finally won out. Although rare in Lapland, the lily of the valley grows in all parts of Finland.

The Swan

The swan is featured as a mythical being in rock drawings, which are thousands of years old, at Lake Onega. One species, the whooper swan, was virtually extinct by the 1950s. In the west, it was hunted as game; in the east, it was held sacred. It was through the efforts of Yrjö Kokko, a veterinarian in Lapland, and a study he made of the bird, that created an awareness of the need for its preservation. Since becoming a protected species, nesting swans are found throughout Finland. The swan is a popular symbol of environmentally safe products.

The Bear

Traditionally the brown bear of the Finnish forest was given the status of respect, but it was also feared and hunted. Initially, bears were hunted with spears; a kill was considered a great feat. As firearms came into greater use, the brown bear became a threatened species, and by the middle of the nineteenth century were essentially found only in the great forests in northern Finland and the eastern border regions. Although they are now considered an endangered species, hunting is still permitted on a limited scale since they can be a threat to livestock and a potential danger to populated areas.

The Birch

In the vote for Finland's national tree, the birch won out handily. Aside from the fact that one-fifth of Finland's forests are mainly birch trees, the "birch bark culture" is a rural Finnish way of life. The birch provided for those skilled in the use of its gifts: birch sap made a healthy drink in the spring; the bark was used for roofing, binding, making baskets, dishes, and other containers, or even birch-bark shoes. Wood of the birch tree was used for buildings, furniture, and tools. Leafy twigs were tied into sauna switches or dried for winter fodder for livestock. Saunas and many homes with woodburning stoves are heated with birch logs. Birch is also an excellent source for the paper fiber industry. Care is given to the renewal of the birch forests. The birch tree, harvested around age fifty years, begins to deteriorate around a hundred, but some can reach an age of 300 years.

The Perch

The most common species of fish in Finland, the perch is found in almost any type of the many waterways in the country, except in the mountainous regions of Lapland. Small in size, the perch can exist in small streams or ponds and big lakes, or even in the brackish water of the Baltic. It is a common catch of the sport fisherman, and is a tasty favorite on the table.

Granite

Most of the bedrock of Finnish topography was formed some 1,800–2,800 million years ago, and the youngest types are about 1,600 years. Some half of the bedrock of Finland is granite. The amounts of different minerals in its composition cause variations in the color. Since the material is widely used in construction and for sculpture, the granite quarries and finishing plants are a large industry. A most unusual and essentially Finnish use of granite is the production of precision cut and finished paper machine rollers, which weigh tens of tons.

HOLIDAYS AND CELEBRATIONS

Since a majority of Finns in the last century were farmers, seasonal changes affected the pattern of life. Over the years, important dates in the farming season combined with church holidays to make up the calendar of traditional celebrations. Finnish Americans enjoy following the major holiday celebrations found in Finland.

INDEPENDENCE DAY

Between "Little Christmas" and Christmas, December 6 is Finland's Independence Day. This is a most important holiday, celebrating the nation's independence gained in 1917. There are parades, flags, music, speeches, and formal and informal gatherings, including a ball at the presidential palace. Almost every household has two blue-and-white candles in the window, lit in the early afternoon since it is dark by three o'clock on this short winter day. Many Finnish-American organizations plan special programs or events to be held on this day.

LUCIA'S DAY

This practice spread from Sweden in the 1920s. On December 13, in the Swedish-speaking schools and homes of Finland, this is a day of enlightenment and goodwill. The day coincides with the shortest day of the year. A national Lucia is chosen by public vote, which is combined with fund raising, usually for the health care organization *Folkhälsan*.

CHRISTMAS
by Clarence W. Ivonen

On Christmas Eve, the cemeteries of Finland glow with the light of countless candles, turning the graves of loved ones into a sparkling message of hope and certainty. It is a beautiful Christmas custom, ideally suited to this northern nation where winter nights are long. Throughout Finland, the trek to the cemetery is made as darkness nears. Evergreen wreaths are placed on the graves. Candles are in hurricane-type lamp shields if necessary. Flaming tar pots burn near memorial markers to the war dead.

The day before Christmas is the big festive day. After the cemeteries are lighted, and following the *joulusauna,* the festive board is served. It may include lutefisk, pork, the traditional rutabaga dish, and casseroles of every sort, rice pudding with a good luck almond for some lucky recipient, or Christmas prune tarts. Then *joulupukki* comes! *Joulupukki* is Finnish for Santa Claus or St. Nicholas, but the word actually translates as "Christmas Goat." In pre-Christian times, someone dressed as a goat or ram went from house to house and tossed small gifts in the door. Today the gift giver dresses as St. Nicholas or Santa, but is called *joulupukki* as in ancient times.

Christmas Day is a day for early morning church services and family reunions. The day after Christmas is St. Stephen's Day, a legal holiday, followed by St. John the Evangelist Day, and Day of the Innocent Children, not legal holidays but observed, at least in the old days, as semi-holidays, when farm dwellers did not do a full day of chores, sometimes holding various bees with feasting and dancing.

An old custom was that of the *tiernapojat* (Starboys). Three young men or boys depicting the wise men went from house to house singing about the three wise men and the Christ Child. They dressed in white robes and cone-shaped hats and carried a wand topped with the Star of Bethlehem. The host family thanked the singers with money or Christmas treats. The custom, which came to Finland from Europe via Sweden, survives now mainly in public performances.

A recent custom is the pre-Christmas secular party by groups, business firms, and clubs, similar to the season's parties in the United States. These are called *pikkujoulu* or "Little Christmas," and first became popular in the 1920s.

The Christmas tree custom was introduced to Finland in 1829. Before that, the principal Christmas decoration, especially in farm dwellings, was the *himmeli* or rye straw mobile of various geometric patterns. The word *himmeli* comes from the Swedish term for heaven. Sometimes it was called *olkikruunu* (straw crown). Straw was a symbol of good fortune and the *himmeli* was hung over the dining table on Christmas Eve. In some areas near Porvoo, the straw mobile was kept up until *Juhannus* or Midsummer to assure good crops. In other areas, the bigger the *himmeli* the better the chances for good fortune. Young girls used to hold *himmeli* bees in the dressing room of a sauna, where moisture would make the thick rye straw more supple for stringing with coarse linen thread. The gathering of young girls attracted young men and the *himmeli* bees became great social times in many villages. Sometimes the *himmeli* was decorated with paper or woolen streamers, paper flowers, eggshells, or bits of mirror. Homes of some Finnish Americans today may have a *himmeli* hanging in a place of honor at Christmastime.

CHRISTOPHER
A Christmas greeting by Bernhard Hillila

This is the traffic-worn roadway
that carried
    the hoof-weary donkey
that carried
    the expectant Virgin
that carried
    the promised Savior
who carried
    the sins of our hate-torn world!

NEW YEAR'S EVE

New Year's Day is a repeat of feasting and gathering, but New Year's Eve is a time for magic. Fortunes may be told by objects hidden in a number of places, often under cups or in puddings. Often tin is melted over a fire and cast into a bucket of cold water. The resulting mold is then held up to cast its shadow, which is then interpreted to foretell the fortune of the coming year. Unmarried girls often foresee a marriage in the casting.

LASKIAINEN (SHROVETIDE)

Laskiainen means descent into Lent, and is celebrated on the Tuesday before Ash Wednesday in Finland. (It's the Finnish version of Fat Tuesday.) Along with the religious significance, it is a celebration of the seasons. Traditionally, there are outdoor activities—sledding, sleigh rides, skiing. There are often special foods and other gatherings. Centuries-old Shrovetide dishes include pea soup, oven pancakes, and Shrovetide buns, somewhat like hot cross buns with delicious (usually cream) fillings.

FRIENDSHIP DAY

Special festivities of peer groups are growing in importance. Age groups, work groups, and different interest groups are creating their own special celebrations. At the end of the 1980s, St. Valentine's Day became part of the Finnish calendar as *Ystävänpäivä*, "Friendship Day." This day is used to promote interests of different organizations and to further charities.

KALEVALA DAY

February 28 is *Kalevala* Day, celebrated all over the country in the spirit of the Finnish national epic poem by Elias Lönnrot, published in 1835. Concerts, poetry recitals, singing, and plays celebrate national pride and appreciation of the Finnish language and heritage.

ST. URHO'S DAY

 St. Urho's Day is an invention of Finnish Americans, who cherish the folkways brought by their forefathers. But one bit of folklore that was lacking was a patron saint such as the one celebrated by the Irish on St. Patrick's Day. So they invented St. Urho. Most all the states have proclaimed March 16 as St. Urho's Day. Costumes of nile green and royal purple are the colors of the day. Thanks are offered to the legendary St. Urho for saving the nonexistent grape crop of Finland from grasshoppers.

EASTER

Easter is the oldest of the church holidays and retains more of its religious character than other church holidays. It is celebrated on the Sunday following the first full moon after the Vernal Equinox. The word for Easter, *pääsiäinen*, means "getting out," referring to Christ leaving the tomb. In the early days, if the sun sparkled at sunrise, it meant that it would be a good year for the crops and berries.

Secular traditions of the season include *virpominen*. Children dress up as Easter witches on Palm Sunday and carry switches made from willow branches, sometimes decorated with paper flowers. They lightly lash at friends and relatives with the magical branch while reciting a charm to ensure good health and success. This tradition is an example of how Christian customs and folk superstitions often merge in Finland. A pre-Easter tradition in many homes is to bring pussy willows, *pajunkissoja*, or other branches indoors for decorations. Some families keep them in a vase, and decorate them with colored eggs or paper flowers.

MIDSUMMER DAY

Midsummer Day is celebrated by Finns on the Saturday between June 20 and 26, near the summer solstice, when the sun is at its highest point in the northern hemisphere. Juhannus, the Festival of St. John the Baptist, is observed on June 24. It is a day to be out-of-doors sailing, swimming, picnicking, and hiking. Homes are decorated with flowers and birches. Dancing and singing around bonfires continue throughout the night. Finnish Americans and Canadian Finns continue to celebrate the day with bonfires and merriment.

MAY DAY

Vappu, May Day happens on the first of May. Every Finn celebrates the spring regardless of how cold it may be. There are parades, brass bands, and singing and dancing to celebrate the coming of summer. It is a celebration that means many different things to many people. There are influences of the workers' movement; groups celebrate other European persuasions; students celebrate graduation. It is a carnival in the streets with Finnish-style enthusiasm.

MOTHER'S DAY

Mother's Day, held the second Sunday in May, acquired national importance in Finland following the Finnish Civil War in 1918, when thousands of war widows were honored on Mother's Day. The Second World War offered yet another reason to continue this tradition, which included the President of Finland in the ceremonies. The custom of honoring Mother in the home with a gift of flowers, cards, and other special attention continues, but the national importance is losing popularity, probably due to the ages of conflict now long relegated to history.

SAMI
INDIGENOUS PEOPLE OF THE NORTH

The Sami region, Lapland, extends from central Norway and Sweden through the northernmost part of Finland, and into the Kola Peninsula. Famed as "the land of the midnight sun," in summer it is light enough to read outdoors at midnight. The reindeer of Lapland inspired Alvar Aalto to design the capital, Rovaniemi, in the shape of reindeer antlers.

There are about 7,000 Sami within the borders of Finland. Sami culture is based on their use of the natural resources of the territory called the Sami Homeland, which is divided into private farms, and the "public lands" controlled by the state. Private lands are used mainly for agriculture, forestry, and some fishing; public lands are used for reindeer herding, fishing, and hunting. About 40 percent of all the reindeer live in the Homeland. A reindeer belongs to the person whose earmark has been cut in its ears. Finnish law does not grant the Sami any special rights to the public lands.

The Sami Parliament is the representative body for the Sami people and territory, which includes four municipalities. The parliament decides how money set aside for the benefit of Sami culture is to be distributed, as well as looks after concerns of the Sami as an indigenous people.

Traditional handcrafts and tourism are a main source of income for some Sami in the Province of Lapland. Wooden reindeer milking bowls, knives, and other products made from reindeer antlers, bone, wood, leather, pewter, thread, and spruce roots are among the typical handcrafted items, known for their natural materials and vibrant colors.

In Rovaniemi, the Gateway to Lapland at the Arctic Circle, the cultures of people living above the Arctic Circle are displayed in the Arktikum Science Museum and the Lapland Provincial Museum. Santa Claus Village is home to Santa's office, post office, shops, and restaurants. (Santa's post office is: Arctic Circle, FIN-96930, Rovaniemi, Finland.) Santa Park highlights the Magic Sleigh Ride (with a stop at Santa's workshop), Puppet Circus, Christmas Carousel, and a multimedia theatre that tells the story of Christmas. Ounasvaara (Ounas Hill) is the site of midsummer as well as winter festivities.

At the northern tip of the Baltic Sea, Kemi features a cruise on the icebreaker Sampo. There is the world's largest Snow Castle, rebuilt each year since 1996, or a stay in a three-story temple of snow, the Snow Hotel, decorated Lapland style with a display of ice furnishings. In northwestern Lapland in Kittilä, the Levi resort is a winter wonderland.

The Inari Sami Museum and Northern Lapland Nature Center in northeastern Finland is a discovery of the rich spiritual heritage and identity of the Finnish Sami. Saariselkä, in the heart of northern Lapland, is complete with activities in a vast area that includes the Urho Kekkonen National Park. Igloo Village offers a unique housing option with fifteen igloos ready for booking. Nearby Tankavaara's Gold Village is the only original gold village in Europe north of the Arctic Circle. The Kaamos Jazz festival takes place around the end of October, the season when the "Northern Lights" may light the sky. In this Land of the Midnight Sun, the "longest summer day" lasts for over two months, when the sun doesn't set for several weeks.

And in all of Samiland there is *yoik,* traditional Sami music, and the rich colorful art and costume of the Sami people.

Photograph by Gerry Kangas

North American Sami Siida *(gathering) at the 59th annual Laskiainen festival, Palo, Minnesota. Some come from as far away as the Canadian Northwest Territories; Toronto, Ontario; and Kautokeino, Norway. Norwegian Sami Johan Mikkel Sara (pictured third from right), who represents his people in the Norwegian Parliament, served as guest dignitary.*

HEIKINPÄIVÄ
MID-WINTER FESTIVAL
HANCOCK, MICHIGAN

Photo courtesy of the Finnish American Reporter

Cheryl Faller, Freda, Michigan, parades in a bear costume she made to represent the Finnish proverb "Karhu kääntää kylkeä." *("The bear rolls over on his side."), which signifies winter is half over. She carries the Finnish flag.*

Photo by Karen Emond, Finnish American Reporter

Maija Stadius shown as the year 2000 "Hankooki Heikki," honorary title for the festival king or queen chosen for his or her contribution to Finnish culture. Maija, a second-grade teacher, teaches Finnish history and language to her students.

Heikinpäivä, St. Henrik's Day, is celebrated on January 19, name day of this extolled bishop of Uppsala and patron saint of Finland. Since the date falls at the halfway mark of winter, there are a variety of folk sayings giving cause to celebrate: *"Karhu kylkeänsä kääntää."* ("The bear rolls onto his other side."); *"Talven selkä poikki."* ("Winter's back is broken."); *"Heikki heinät jakaa."* ("Heikki divides the hay.") The latter refers to a time when farmers take stock of the hay, grains, and other commodities to make sure enough is left to survive the rest of winter.

Hancock, Michigan's "welcome" to mid-winter is a grand celebration in the Finnish tradition, drawing hundreds of spirited participants in this

22–

break in the winter doldrums. Jim Kurtti, co-chairman of the Finnish Theme Committee for the 2002 celebration, says that tickets for the traditional Finnish Buffet on Heikinpäivä Eve, served at Finlandia Hall, Finlandia University, were an early sell-out.

The parade on Saturday morning is a show of Finnish and Sami culture and pride. Entries range from a group of children from Salolampi with full-sized paper maché Moomintrolls to FinPro's portable sauna. Among the dignitaries and festival royalty are St. Urho, St. Henrik, "the bear," and Heikki Lunta (Snow Henry), Copper Country modern folk hero. The legend of Heikki Lunta was born during a mild winter in 1970 that threatened to curtail normal Michigan activities requiring snow. David Riutta, a representative of Hancock radio WMPL, inspired by the music of a popular country western song, wrote the lyrics to the "Heikki Lunta Snow Dance Song." The fictional hero was said to live in the backwoods of Tapiola, and was reported to have the ability to do a dance that would cause the snow to fall. The WMPL team took the song to the airwaves, and miraculously it began to snow and snow and snow. Some said that maybe Heikki Lunta danced too much. Other popular events include the *Tori* (market); the reindeer camp; a house and sculptures of snow; a ski race; whip-sledding; cooking and/or weaving classes; a Finn Hall-style dance, and the challenging "polar bear plunge," a jump into the frigid waters of the Portage Canal!

That's Finnish *sisu!*

Photo by Karen Emond, Finnish American Reporter

Traditional Finnish crown wedding procession

FINNISH-AMERICAN FOLK DANCERS
GRAND FEST 2000, TORONTO

Joan Liffring-Zug Bourret photographs

KALEVALA VILLAGE AT KUHMO

Cranberry sauce is served at the midsummer feast at the Kalevala Village Hotel at Kuhmo. *This sauce reminds many Finnish-American visitors to Finland of the fruit sauces of their childhoods. The village represents the old Karelian way of life and culture with exhibitions, artisan displays, and demonstrations.*

Gerry Kangas photographs

Orthodox Church Heinävesi, Finland

Statue commemorates the Karelian matriarch. Wise older women, keepers of the culture, were dirge singers.

The Valamo Monastery is a center for the Orthodox Christian faith. More than 800 years ago the monastery was on an island in Lake Ladoga in Russia. In 1940, 200 monks moved to the area of Heinävesi. The monastery is open year-round offering guest facilities, shops, and boat cruises. The monastery church is shown below.

Gerry Kangas photographs

THE CRAFT *TORI* AT OULU, FINLAND

Gerry Kangas
photograph

SALOLAMPI

Weaving at Salolampi

Main building, Salolampi Finnish Language Village

SALOLAMPI
FINNISH LANGUAGE VILLAGE

In northern Minnesota on Turtle River Lake, there is a bit of Finland on a 40-acre site of birch and pine. The Salolampi Finnish Language Village is one of twelve Concordia Language Villages. Salolampi, Finnish for "Lake in the Woods," is located near Bemidji, Minnesota. The handsome main building, Jyringin Talo, is patterned after the architecturally historic railway station in Jyväskylä, Finland. Finnish architectural style is apparent throughout the village in four imported log cabins and a sauna, two additional cabins, crafts and staff buildings. Building Salolampi was the heartfelt work of the Salolampi Foundation at a cost of $2 million, made possible by hundreds of Finnish-American donors and Concordia College.

Finnish villagers are immersed in the Finnish language and culture. Villagers learn the language through a wide variety of Finnish cultural activities: arts and crafts, sports, dancing and singing, foods, and business. Evening programs celebrate Finnish heritage, holidays and folklore, as well as exploring environmental and political issues. Salolampi adult weeks are also offered each spring, fall, and winter when the young people are not in session.

One-week, two-week, and four-week sessions are offered during June and July. Youth from throughout the United States attend Salolampi each summer. Children from ages 7 to 18 are eligible to apply. The four-week session provides high school language credit to villagers in grades 9–12. Salolampi's enthusiastic staff of Finns and Americans includes counselors, accredited teachers, and program leaders. Scholarship support to villagers is provided from donated scholarships and gifted funds to the Salolampi Foundation.

For enrollment information contact:
Salolampi Foundation: info@finnsonline.org (www.finnsonline.org)
or P.O. Box 14480; Minneapolis, MN; 55414
or Concordia Language Villages (www.cord.org/dept/clv/)
at (800) 222-4750.

—Marlene Banttari

A Way of Life: Sauna

*"Anger cools in the sauna,
Resentment fades away."*

—a Finnish couplet from
The Sauna Is... by Bernhard Hillila

Finland has 5.1 million people and 1.7 million saunas. There are public saunas in hotels, factories, and hospitals. During World War II, Finnish soldiers built saunas at the front lines.

The idea of the sauna was not new nor invented by the Finns. Many European nations had similar bathing rituals in the past: the Greeks, Romans, and Turks are known for them. In rural Mexico, steam baths heated from the outside are used even today. The American-Indian sweat lodge is used for medicinal purposes rather than bathing.

The Finnish sauna has a long history that has stayed with the Finns. Farm people often built the sauna first—living in it while building their home. The sauna served as a place for many functions, such as giving birth and bloodletting (cupping), that were performed there well into the twentieth century. According to the Finnish-American Heritage organization of Minneapolis, the last birth of a baby in a Minnesota sauna occurred near Carlton in 1938.

The sauna culture has spread throughout the world. In America, saunas acquired much wider popularity when one was installed at the 1960 Winter Olympics at Squaw Valley, California. President John F. Kennedy built one at the White House.

Typically a sauna consists of a dressing room, a steam room with wooden benches, and a stove of hot glowing stones heating the room to 190° to 280° F. Splashing water on the stones *(kiuas)* makes the sauna steamier. The Finnish word for the super hot vapor created from the stones is *"löyly,"* which is described as the spirit of the sauna. Some bathers gently beat themselves with wet, leafy birch twigs *(vihta)* to stimulate circulation. Following a hot sauna, bathers often jump into the nearest lake or swimming pool, and then repeat the process. Saunas for men and women are usually separate. Inviting guests for a sauna is as common as inviting them to a meal.

The essentials for any sauna are basically: a wooden structure, rocks that can be heated, hot and cold air, and hot and cold water. The ideal sauna is a small building made of logs, facing the sunset near a lakeshore. Architecture and design have been adapted through the years, but along with function, in keeping with the sauna "mystique," construction should be simple and rustic. The heat source in the original sauna was a "smoke stove" still in use today by many sauna purists. Instead of a chimney, there is a smoke hole in the ceiling, and the sauna is permeated with the incense of wood smoke. A stove with chimney was introduced to reduce the risk of fire. The electric stove followed. Most American saunas are heated by gas or electricity, since they are usually built within a main residence.

The sauna "way of life" supports thorough cleansing, physiological conditioning, and relaxation—with a sense of pleasure and well-being. Author Bernhard Hillila aptly describes the relaxing effects of the sauna: "One seems to let off steam figuratively as he takes in steam literally. . . . If genius is 10 percent inspiration and 90 percent perspiration, try thinking through your problems in a sauna!"

Erick and Kristina Nelimark Sauna
National Historic Register Site, Embarrass, Minnesota

KALEVAN KIRVESMIEHET
THE AXEMEN OF KALEVA

by Martti Mattson

For the American Bicentennial, the Duluth Lodge of the Knights of Kaleva, a Finnish-American fraternal organization, decided to make a display of log-building methods of Finnish ancestors. It was a contribution to the Summer Festival of the Western Lake Superior Region Finnish-American Bicentennial Committee.

Skill with the broadaxe was a ticket to immediate employment for many Finns who came to this country, but the advent of the small sawmill ended the need for hand-hewn timbers or hand-cut door and window frames. The craft of a thousand years was extinct. How could a complete sauna be built as our ancestors would have done it?

Of the tools needed, a few were peculiar to the trade in Finland: the broadaxe *(piilu)*, scriber *(vararauta)*, plumbboard *(luotilauta)*. We were able to find tools, but we wound up making scribers and log dogs *(jaaki* or *hollihaka)*, broadaxe handles, plus chisels and mallets. We began to feel the affinity for wood. . . . The Axemen of Kaleva *(Kalevan Kirvesmiehet)* were ready.

In November 1975, we cut, felled, and hauled out some choice fir logs. . . . hewed them to size. . . . We fitted the logs to each other by layers, cutting the dovetail corners and the door and window openings. The 10 x 12-foot building began to take shape. We dismantled the structure log by log, marking each one. . . .

The crowning achievement was a call to Washington, D.C., to the Festival of American Folklife at the Smithsonian Institution. We hauled about three and a half tons of fresh fir logs from Minnesota to the Mall in the shadow of the Washington Monument and built an 8 x 8-foot sauna in less than a week. At the end of the festival, the sauna was sold at auction to a Washingtonian. It is now in regular use in the historic section of Washington, D.C., a mere six blocks from our nation's capitol.

NOTABLE AND FAMOUS FINNS

CARL GUSTAV MANNERHEIM

After gaining its independence, Finland called on Carl Gustav Mannerheim (1867–1951) twice to head its armed forces, and twice asked him to serve as chief of state.

In 1917, newly independent Finland had won recognition from the new communist government of Russia, but Finnish Communists began a civil war, taking Helsinki and much of southern Finland. The new Finnish government asked Mannerheim to command its armed forces. He organized his army in western Finland and defeated the Communists in three months. In 1918, after Germany's World War I surrender,

C.G. Mannerheim Statue
Helsinki

the Finnish government asked Mannerheim to serve as regent (head of state) pending adoption of a Constitution for a Finnish Republic. In 1931, at age sixty-four, after more than a decade as a private citizen, Mannerheim became chairman of the Finnish Defense Council, to be commander in chief in case of war. War came November 20, 1939. Finnish troops fought heroically, but on March 12, 1940, Finland had to cede to Russia much of southeastern Finland, including the city of Viipuri.

When Germany attacked the Soviet Union on June 22, 1941, Finland was drawn into the "Continuation War." Much of East Karelia was retaken, but when Russian troops broke through the lines in June 1944, the government again asked Mannerheim to become head of state. He accepted, ordered the German army to leave Finland, and sued for peace. Russia again took much territory, leaving the borders as they are today, but Finland remained independent.

JEAN SIBELIUS

"Music is on a higher level than everything else in this world."
—Jean Sibelius

The strains of Sibelius seem wafted on cool fall breezes from the free Polar north through the pines of Finland. His aim and his accomplishment was to create music that echoes in tone the deep values of the culture, the people, the geography, the lore, and the freedom of Finland.

Jean Sibelius (1865–1957) studied music avidly, and was a violin virtuoso as well as a composer. He began his study of music performance and composition in Finland and continued later in Berlin and Vienna, returning to Finland in 1891. His most celebrated national work, *Finlandia*, written in 1899, was arousing and inspiring. Many of his works were inspired by his readings of the *Kalevala*, and in some degree the folk music of Karelia. The main driving force in his classical style was a purely musical continuous growth.

In 1904, he built a house outside Helsinki in Järvenpää, where he spent the rest of his life with his wife and daughters. This was a beginning of change in his personal life. Away from the city, his music reflected a modification in his thinking. A fastidious dresser, Sibelius cherished youth. Spotting gray hairs at age forty, he kept his head shaved the rest of his life.

In 1951, the Finnish government sponsored a festival of his music that became an annual event. The entire nation helped him celebrate his ninetieth birthday. The influence of his work was profound, especially on Scandinavian, English, and American composers.

After his death, his picture appeared on Finnish stamps, and a 26-foot abstract sculpture, the Sibelius Monument, was erected in his memory in Sibelius Park in Helsinki. The monument also hailed the 50th anniversary of Finnish independence.

ALVAR AALTO

*"We should work for simple, good, undecorated things,
but things that are in harmony with the human being."*
—Alvar Aalto

Alvar Aalto (1898–1976), one of the great architects of the twentieth century, designed buildings, furniture, and glassware. Aalto's work—useful, space-saving, and tasteful—is popular and recognizable.

One of his first buildings to gain international acclaim as a major achievement was the Paimio Tuberculosis Sanatorium. Along with required hospital technology, the emphasis on the human side, such as sunlit balconies, the aesthetics of view, and furnishings are notable. Aalto and his first wife, Aino Marsio, designed the furnishings for this building and several others. In 1935 they founded Artek, which continues to produce furnishings.

Three-legged stools that stack and stackable chairs are well-known Aalto designs. Aalto furniture is usually crafted from lightweight, light-colored natural wood, often birch. Even his kitchenware is practical—stacking plates and bowls.

His attention to varied forms and material created an environment to be experienced through the senses, not just the eyes. "Aalto" means "wave," a form that was almost his signature. The Aalto wave was predominant in his Finnish Pavilion at the 1939 New York World's Fair, incorporating native landscape with undulating profiles of Finnish lakes.

Aalto painted throughout his life as an aesthetic exercise. The techniques applied in collage resulted in astonishing architectural form. He designed buildings in Finland, Germany, Denmark, Italy, and the United States. It has been said that Finland was with him wherever he went, but his greatest works were on Finnish soil. Notably among the finest is Finlandia Hall, the waterfront cultural center in Helsinki.

Paavo Nurmi

"The Flying Finn"

Paavo Nurmi (1897–1973), also called "the Phantom Finn" by newspaper writers, was the world's greatest long-distance runner. Nurmi won six Olympic gold medals: at the 1920 games at Antwerp—the 10,000-meter run and the 10,000-meter cross country race; at the 1924 games at Paris—the 1,500-meter run, the 5,000-meter run, and the 10,000-meter cross country race; at the 1928 games at Amsterdam—the 10,000-meter run.

On an American tour after the 1924 Olympics, he spread the fame of Finland and set thirty-eight indoor world records. From 1920 to 1932, he set twenty outdoor world records. His 1923 world record run of one mile in 4 minutes 10.4 seconds stood for eight years.

Following his success at the Paris Olympics, one news reporter facetiously noted: "Every single person in Finland goes through, day after day, the ordeal of talking in Finnish. After that, why should anyone be surprised what any Finn accomplishes?"

Nurmi had an idol of his own in Johannes Kolehmainen, a bricklayer, who it was said, "ran Finland onto the map," winning the 5,000- and 10,000-meter runs and the 8,000-cross country in the Sixth Olympiad held in Stockholm in 1912. Kolehmainen had helped Nurmi train for the 1924 Paris Olympic track events.

In 1924 during Nurmi's tour of the United States, President Calvin Coolidge invited him to the White House, and many years later President Lyndon Johnson asked if he might meet Nurmi during a visit to Finland. Worldwide admiration for this Olympic legend was apparent in "Olympic" proportion at the 1952 Helsinki games, when Nurmi, at age fifty-five, dashed into the stadium bearing the torch to light the Olympic flame.

Editor's Note: In recent years, the Embarrass, Minnesota, track team, winners of many trophies, were called "The Flying Finns." They were coached by Ed Hendrickson.

ELIEL SAARINEN

Architect and Teacher

Eliel Saarinen (1873–1950), inspired architect and teacher, brought the best of modern Finnish design to America, exerting a more profound influence than perhaps is yet realized. In his first forty-five years, Finland was a Russian duchy. The next five years, Finland was a nation. From age fifty to his death, he lived in the United States.

In 1900, Saarinen and two others submitted the winning design for the Finnish Pavilion at the Paris World's Fair in 1904. The same three won the competition for design of the Helsinki Central Railway Station. The three had begun construction, in 1902, of Hvitträsk, a thirty-eight room granite and wood structure overlooking the lake of the same name eighteen miles from Helsinki. By 1907, his two partners were gone, but Saarinen and others lived and worked and studied architecture and design projects. Hvitträsk has since become a national shrine.

In 1904, far away in Bloomfield Township, a suburb of Detroit, Michigan, George C. Booth, a newspaper publisher, bought an estate that came to be known as Cranbrook. Booth wanted the property to be used for the public good, and when Saarinen came to the United States in 1923 and met Booth, the idea of the Cranbrook Academy of Art became a reality. Today it is recognized as the fountainhead from which modern Finnish design entered the American scene, and for itself as an architectural gem. It was a natural extension of Hvitträsk.

Eliel Saarinen designed Nikander Hall at Suomi College (now Finlandia University) in Hancock, Michigan. Other works done in collaboration with his son Eero include campus plans and certain buildings for Brandeis University, Waltham, Massachusetts; Antioch College, Yellow Springs, Ohio; and Christ Lutheran Church, Minneapolis.

EERO SAARINEN

A Creative Spirit

Innovative and imaginative, Eero Saarinen (1910–1961) was one of the great architects of the twentieth century. Each assignment was a new and different challenge. He believed that function influences, but does not dictate form. His results were strikingly pleasing and remarkably functional.

Eero was son of architect Eliel Saarinen; his mother was a sculptor and a weaver. At age twelve, Eero won a Swedish contest for matchstick design. At about the same time, his father won $20,000 as second prize in the *Chicago Tribune's* competition for design of the Tribune tower. This prize brought the family to the United States.

Eero studied at his father's inspired Cranbrook Academy of Art near Detroit, Michigan; at La Grande Chaumiere in Paris; and at Yale University, graduating in 1934.

At age twenty-six, Eero began practicing with his father and teaching at Cranbrook. In 1948, he won the $50,000 grand prize for design of the Jefferson Westward Expansion Memorial National Historic Site, the prominent feature of which is the Gateway Arch, sometimes called the St. Louis Arch. Cranbrook sculpture student Joe Roper recalled that the award committee thought the prize design was by the father, Eliel.

Also in 1948, with his father, Eliel, age seventy-five, and Eero, thirty-eight, it was mutually agreed that the son, and not the father, would be in charge of a project that had mushroomed to become a $100 million complex of buildings for the General Motors Technical Center at Warren, Michigan.

Eero Saarinen's career was cut short by brain cancer at age fifty-one. He did not live to see some of his best work completed. His life was a major contribution to architectural design, a harvest of creative spirit and *sisu,* which he defined as "extended guts."

Gateway Arch designed by Eero Saarinen
Jefferson Westward Expansion Memorial National Historic Site, St. Louis, Missouri

Sites of Saarinen's architecture

1954 University of Michigan, Ann Arbor: Master Plan.

1945–55 Drake University, Des Moines, Iowa: Campus plan, Pharmacy Building, Dormitories and Dining Hall.

1952–55 Irwin Union Bank and Trust Company, Columbus, Indiana.

1952–55 Massachusetts Institute of Technology (MIT), Cambridge: Kresge Auditorium and Chapel.

1948–56 General Motor's Technical Center, Warren, Michigan.

1953–57 Milwaukee County War Memorial Center, Milwaukee, Wisconsin.

1958 Ingalls Hockey Rink, Yale University, New Haven, Connecticut.

1954–58 Emma Hartman Noyes House, Vassar College, Poughkeepsie, New York.

1953–58 Concordia Senior College, Fort Wayne, Indiana: Campus Plan.

1955–58 University of Chicago: Women's Dormitory and Dining Hall.

1956–59 International Business Machines, Rochester, Minnesota.

1955–59 United States Embassy, Oslo, Norway.

1955–60 United States Embassy, London, England.

1956–60 University of Chicago Law School.

1957–60 University of Pennsylvania, Philadelphia: Women's Dormitories.

1957–61 International Business Machines, Yorktown, New York: Thomas J. Watson Research Center.

1958–62 Yale University: Ezra Stiles and Morse Colleges.

1956–62 TransWorld Airways (TWA) Terminal, John F. Kennedy International Airport, New York City.

1958–62 Dulles (Washington, D.C.) International Airport, Chantilly, Virginia.

1957–63 Deere & Company Headquarters, Moline, Illinois.

1963 Vivian Beaumont Theater, Lincoln Center, New York City.

1959–63 North Christian Church, Columbus, Indiana.

1960–64 Columbia Broadcasting System (CBS) Building, New York City.

1948–64 Jefferson Westward Expansion Memorial (St. Louis Arch), St. Louis, Missouri.

–39

THE FINNISH TRADITION OF LITERATURE

A CELEBRATION OF LANGUAGE

by Richard Impola

At a Finlandia Foundation picnic in upstate New York, a group of Finns and Finnish Americans gather to celebrate Midsummer Day with a picnic. A tenor in training at the Metropolitan opera sings a beautiful Finnish folk song and is heartily applauded. Then a man rises and recites a poem about the occasion and is greeted with equal applause.

In both the song and the poem, the audience responds to the beauty of the language. One hears in the words the voice of nature itself, which is perhaps one reason why Finns still love poetry. Their love of nature is proverbial—the cottage in the woods on the shore of a lake is every Finn's dream of paradise. And their love of poetry dates back some thousands of years to the oral tradition of *Kalevala* verse, which is no less than the literature of a people in poetic form. Love of nature and love of poetry go hand in hand.

Many of the people at the picnic are urban Finns—two busloads from New York City and Long Island, hardly a bucolic or poetic environment. Yet their emotional response to the poetry is intense and genuine. In verse, Finns still find the most satisfying expression of their feelings and their sense of beauty.

Richard Impola, a retired college professor and a native of Michigan's Upper Peninsula, has been active as a translator of many major Finnish literary works. He received the Inger Sjoberg prize for translation and the contract from the Finnish Literature Information Center to translate Under the North Star *and other titles in Vaino Linna's classic trilogy.*

FINNS LOVE POETRY

by Bernhard Hillila

Finland is a wordstruck nation.

To begin with, oral poetry has deep roots in Finnish culture. Finland is the only country which has a national holiday commemorating its national epic—the *Kalevala*. It is remembered on *Kalevala* Day, February 28.

Let's face it: Where Nature is most alluring, she may elicit much poetic response. Finland has a wealth of forests and lakes beneath a high sky with pure clouds and northern lights.

Furthermore, the written word became very important to Finns after the Protestant Reformation of the early 1500s. The authority for salvation became a book (the Bible) rather than a person (the Pope). That meant emphasizing literacy in general as well as reading the Bible itself, which is one-third poetry. Scripture has also inspired countless hymns and spiritual songs.

Finns in America have continued their love affair with poetry. Much poetry has been printed in Finnish newspapers and religious periodicals. Poetry has also been prominent at programs and festivals in churches and halls. Such poetry can be by widely recognized authors, but it is also often poetry written by common laborers who are members of a hall or a congregation—participants in a particular evening's program.

Also, it should be noted that the Finnish language is unusually poetic, with soft consonants, a wealth of vowels, plus much rhyme arising from matching case endings.

Professor Emeritus of Education at Valparaiso University in Indiana, Bernhard Hillila is also a Lutheran minister. He devotes his time to poetry, lecturing, conducting workshops, and writing (three books and over 100 poems published in journals and anthologies). In addition to his own writing, Professor Hillila translates from Finnish to English. He was the Finlandia Foundation 1997 Performer of the Year.

The *Kalevala*

by Aili Jarvenpa

The *Kalevala*, national epic of Finland, is the spark that awakened the national spirit of the Finnish people. It gave them a belief in the possibilities of Finland as a nation for the Finns. It gave them confidence in their own language and contributed to the development of Finnish literature.

Composed orally over centuries by unlettered singers, mostly from Karelia, the poems of the *Kalevala* were collected in the field by Elias Lönnrot, a country doctor and literary scholar. He edited and published them in 1835 and again in 1849, in a longer, final version. The *Kalevala* consists of fifty runos (epic narrative poems) and more than 22,000 verses. The epic has its heroes, including Väinämöinen, eternal sage and singer as well as creator of the kantele; Ilmarinen, the eternal smith, and the reckless Lemminkäinen. Female figures include Ilmatar, the tragic Aino, and Louhi, the Mistress of the North Farm.

The men and women in the *Kalevala* are energetic and imaginative skilled craftsmen: shipwrights, blacksmiths, goldsmiths. Fine fabrics are woven, fine jewels esteemed. Music is an important part of their lives. They honor and praise all beauty, whether a bird, a tree, or a young maiden. The poems recount feuds between the people of Kaleva and Pohjola, and the long quest for the Sampo, a magic object forged by Ilmarinen.

The poems give a vivid picture of early peasant life, and have served as a guide to values, traditions, beliefs, and customs of the Finnish people. The *Kalevala* has been a source of inspiration to many Finnish artists, resulting in several major works by composer Sibelius, paintings by Gallen-Kallela, and poetry by Eino Leino.

In 1985, to commemorate the 150th anniversary of the publication of the *Kalevala*, numerous celebrations and seminars were held in Finnish-American communities and colleges and universities.

The *Kalevala* has been translated into forty-six languages.

MINNA CANTH, HEROINE
(1844–1897)

by Inkeri Väänänen-Jensen

As a student in a teachers' seminary,
She married the science professor.
Putting aside her own "idealistic pursuits"
As she called them,
She now began the tasks
Which went against her nature:
Keeping house,
Preparing meals,
Doing needlework,
Taking care of her husband,
Being an obedient wife,
Never expressing her own opinions,
For her husband's will was law in all things.
She said, "I was looked upon as a nobody."

But then one day
She dared express her own opinions.
Surprised, her husband learned to accept them,
For she was usually proved to be right.
And he developed an unshakable faith
In her good judgment.
As a result,
She began to write
About women's rights.
But it was too soon,
And nobody listened.
It was 1875—in Finland.

Her soul became distressed.
"Women are too feminine, too patient,
Too docile, too forbearing, too softhearted.
In a way, too Christian."

"Nordic women," she also wrote,
"Are quiet, faithful, meek,
Patient, obedient servants
To their husbands and children.
Not because they consider it their duty,
But simply because
They're cowards and are confused."

Minna Canth was a writer and social activist. The ideals she championed seemed radical for the times, but her work contributed to change. Finnish women were among the first to obtain the right to vote, in 1906.

Johan Ludvig Runeberg

Finnish National Poet Johan Ludvig Runeberg (1804–1877) was born into a Swedish-speaking family in Pietarsaari, on the shores of the Gulf of Bothnia. At the age of eight, he entered school in Oulu; he later studied at the University of Åbo in Turku. Out of economic need, he interrupted his studies and took a job as a tutor to a family in central Finland. This acquaintance with ordinary Finnish-speaking people strongly influenced his later work. Eventually continuing his studies at the University of Helsinki, his first collection of poems, *Dikter*, appeared in 1830, reflecting his love of Finland's landscape and the inhabitants of the backwoods. He portrayed poverty and misery, but gave his characters the dignity of *sisu*. His great body of writings ranged from social treatises to hymns. The first poem "Vårt land," (Maamme), in his 1846 *Fänrik Ståls Sågner*, became the Finnish national anthem, set to music by Fredrik Pacius in 1848.

Frans Eemil Sillanpää

Finnish Nobel Laureate Frans Eemil Sillanpää (1888–1964), known for his lyrical prose about the Finnish people and landscape, received the Nobel Prize for Literature in 1939. Born to parents who suffered the loss of children, their crops, and animals to the elements of the croft region of the Hämeenkyrö Parish, Frans was the sole surviving child. Farm children attended a circuit school, but Sillanpää was recognized as a bright student, leading to his enrollment in a regular school. By various means he continued his education in the sciences, but when financial resources ran out, he returned to his home on the croft. Here he wrote and had published his first short story under a pen name. He then became known in the literary world of Helsinki, and was given an advance to expand the story to a book—the start of a series of wonderful events leading to the Nobel Prize. The University of Helsinki conferred an honorary doctorate on Sillanpää in 1936.

TOVE JANSSON,
CREATOR OF THE MOOMINTROLLS

"Every children's book should have a path in it where the writer stops and the child goes on. A threat or a delight that can never be explained. A face never revealed."

—Tove Jansson
in *Moominvalley,*
ed. by Mirja Kivi, 1998

Tove Jansson (1914–2001), writer, painter, and illustrator, is known to millions of children and adults as the creator of the world of the Moomintrolls and their friends. Born in Helsinki to artist parents, bohemian studio life in the city and summers in the Porvoo islands in the Gulf of Finland formed the backdrop for the Moomin books.

Jansson became an accomplished artist before beginning a career as a cartoonist. She contributed her first art to magazines when she was fifteen. The Moomintroll characters were introduced in the 1940s. She began drawing a comic strip for the *London Evening News* in 1953, which eventually was read in forty countries.

Originally written in Swedish, the Moomin tales reflect characteristics of the artistic Jansson family's Swedish-speaking minority heritage—art, creativity, and tolerance. In *Moominvalley* in November (1970), Jansson says, "Life is like a river. Some people sail on it slowly, some quickly, and some capsize."

These stories have been translated into many languages, and have been dramatized for different media: television, theatre, opera, film, and radio. The Moomin Museum opened in Tampere in 1987. There are over 2,000 items in the Moominvalley collection at the Tampere Art Museum. A popular visiting place is Moomin World in Naantali.

Jansson has received numerous awards as an artist as well as the most prestigious honors in literature.

FINNISH FOLK ARTS

RYIJY (TAPESTRIES)

The name *ryijy* originated with the Scandinavian word *rya,* which means "thick cloth." The decorative *ryijy* rug is an art form unique to Finland. In the late 1800s, *ryijy* rug-weaving developed as a folk art. Some of the most beautiful tapestries were woven then.

Ryijys date from as early as the ninth century. Similar in nature to a knotted Persian carpet, the *ryijy* knots are further apart and are much larger and longer. Originally woven for use as coverlets and bedding, they were mainly in natural colors, white, grey, and black. Some tones of yellow, red, green, and blue were introduced with vegetable dyes. Later, aniline dyes added another dimension of color and design.

The use of color and pattern is especially unique to the Finnish *ryijy.* Dating back to the 1700s, a *ryijy* was often used as a prayer rug during wedding ceremonies; the tapestry was then hung for display in the couple's home. *Ryijy* weavers traveled with their looms throughout the villages and towns getting commissions to weave a *ryijy* for special occasions. Different regions had designs specific to the event and colors specific to the local plants for dyes. Designs were often geometric shapes and florals, or figures of humans, animals, or birds. A very typical motif was the Tree of Life signifying family heritage.

Today *ryijy*-making techniques include new fibers such as paper string, available in hundreds of colors, as is the traditional wool. They are designed for a multitude of places and purposes, but each is an individual work of art.

FOLK PAINTING

Koristemaalaus, folk painting in Finland, dates back centuries. Folk painting appeared in everyday life in Finland in the late eighteenth century, centering on decoration of furniture and objects such as clocks and trunks. Paintings on many of the objects were "greetings" or commemorative text of some occasion surrounded with ornamental illustration. Suzanne Koski, Colorado folk artist, notes that although there are influences of Swedish, Russian and Karelian folk art, *koristemaalaus* has its own unique character.

Wood Carving and Sculpture

Wood is very much a part of Finnish character; it represents the values of old traditions. The abundant forests provided material for homes, functional furnishings and utensils, and ornamental decor. The combination of peasant tradition and contemporary design has placed Finland in the forefront of design and production of wood products.

Finnish flora, fauna, and mythology were stylized in carved relief or modeled sculpture. Bears, squirrels, pine trees, cones, and different leaves were favored subjects for ornaments. Domestic utensils were an essential craft of the woodcarver. Many skilled Finnish-American artisans continue to produce functional and decorative works today. The advent of the chainsaw has given a new dimension to the size of wood sculpture.

Lastutöitä and Himmeli

The Finnish term *lastutöitä* translates as "lastuwork," the art of using pine shavings to create ornamental works. Designs are generally determined by the creator, but many traditional designs reflect the flora and fauna, such as birds and fish.

The traditional straw mobile, *himmeli*, hung in most Finnish homes at Christmas, is a unique craft of weaving and stitching straw with strong linen thread. Designs range from simple to very intricate. Classes are conducted to teach this distinctive art.

Folk Costumes

The national costume adopts many elements of the folk costumes which were worn by ordinary people with weaving skills and artistic instincts in their home-loomed clothing. Woven from wool with cotton warp, the colorful stripes were the colors and design of more elegant fabrics of the time. The wool was dyed with natural pigments. The costumes of different provinces and regions each had distinct designs and parts. *Kansallispukuraati* has advanced the authentication of provincial costumes. The Lahti-based firm, Helmi Vuorelma, catalogues some 120 women's provincial costumes, and suits for men from twenty-four regions, plus child-size adaptations.

Folk Music, Singing, and Dancing

Few nations have a national culture so rich in the tradition of folk music. A part of the official government cultural policy, there are service, publicity, and research institutions dedicated to folk music, along with several societies and amateur organizations. The famed Sibelius Music Academy has a folk music department; a state-supported folk music band was founded in 1986.

Rune singing in *Kalevala* style and instrumental music with the five-string kantele, the *jouhikko* (a type of bowed lyre), and wind instruments are noted as the oldest expression of performance music. A later style is described as that of peasant culture, or fiddler music.

A revival of folk music came in the 1960s when new musicians joined the old fiddlers, and hundreds of groups were formed, performing traditional music as well as adapting the old to the new. One of Europe's largest folk music festivals takes place in July in the tiny Ostrobothnian municipality of Kaustinen.

Folk dancing is rooted in the same traditions as folk music in Finland. Finnish folk dancing is made up of many elements which have been combined and transformed by the people.

Many Finnish-American organizations get together to share traditional as well as couples' social dances. In the Minneapolis-St. Paul, Minnesota, Finnish community, the group known as "Finn Hall" or "Minnesota Pelimannit" often accompanies the Twin-Cities' folk dance group "Kisarit." The diversity of their performance ranges from Finnish *polkkas, humppas,* and *jenkkas* to waltzes and tangos.

That singing is an important part of the cultural heritage of Finns and Finnish Americans is evident in the many choirs and choruses. Notable among these are the Järvenpää Singers, a group of fifty-five from northern Minnesota and Wisconsin, who meet in Duluth for weekly rehearsals. They perform frequently at area ethnic events and have performed at FinnFests in both the U.S. and Canada. Almost all of their music is sung in Finnish.

THE KANTELE

Joyce Hakala, director of "Koivun Kaiku"

Americans' interest in Finland's traditional folk instrument, the kantele, greatly increased since the mid-1960s when Joyce Hakala first began as a solo performer, playing her grandfather's forty-one-string instrument. After a trip to Finland and purchase of a five-string kantele, Hakala, in 1985, became the founder and director of "Koivun Kaiku" (Echo of the Birch), an ensemble of five to ten players of the kantele in all sizes and traditions, as well as other types of instruments.

The group performs throughout the United States as well as in Finland. Recordings, workshops, and performances have revitalized kantele traditions in America. Hakala's book *Memento of Finland: A Musical Legacy* contains history of the kantele and presents the legacy from immigrant players in stories, facts, and music. She was honored by the Kalevala Society of Finland for her efforts to promote Finnish traditions and was a Finlandia Foundation Performer of the year.

MELVIN KANGAS

Adapted from original article by John Gagnon.

"The kantele is an instrument peculiar unto itself," says musician Melvin Kangas, who composes and likes to adapt all kinds of music to the kantele.

The kantele is rooted in ancient Finnish folk music. It is "a box with strings going across it," Kangas says. The oldest model he has seen has five strings. His own instrument, custom-made by a Finnish craftsman, has thirty-six strings.

In 1974, Melvin Kangas knocked on the door of Ulla Katajavuori in Helsinki, Finland, ready to take lessons from the world's most accomplished kantele player. After many long hours, she told Kangas: "You will become a very good kantele player." Since then Kangas has performed all over the United States and Finland. He pioneered the use of the kantele with a full orchestra.

"It's a very difficult instrument to play," he explained, "and it's like no other instrument. I took harp lessons thinking it would help me play the kantele. It didn't, nor did the piano."

Originally from Tapiola, Michigan, Kangas is a performance musician as well as a teacher at Finlandia University (formerly Suomi College). He says music is a universal language that bridges cultural differences with the ease of a lilting note wafting through the air.

Photo Courtesy of the Clatsop County Historical Society
Liisa Penner contributed this photograph of a musical band of Finnish boys. (early 1900s, Astoria, Oregon)

Ameriikan Poijat
Boys of America

Photo courtesy Paul Niemisto

The Finnish brass septet (called *torviseitsikko* in Finnish) has its roots in the late nineteenth century. Musicians who played in army bands took their music and instruments home with them and formed brass bands in their home communities. These seven-piece brass bands provided live music for events ranging from dance halls to funerals, adapting the music as it developed over time to include folk, tango, cabaret music, and jazz. Founded in 1990, *Ameriikan Poijat* (Boys of America) has included American-born descendants of Finnish immigrants who are musicians and teachers from Minnesota and Michigan. Membership has included Director Paul Niemisto, professor of music at St. Olaf College, Northfield, Minnesota (seated above, right); Russell Pesola; Don Hakala; Karl Hill Kortesmaki; Brian Borovsky; Denise Pesola; Eric Kiltinen; and Eric Peterson. They have toured throughout the United States and Finland, and are supported by prestigious grants and awards from various endowment funds, including the Finlandia Foundation.

FINNISH-AMERICAN HERITAGE

Excerpts from My Story, Inkeri's Journey

BEING FINNISH IN AMERICA
by Inkeri Väänänen-Jensen

. . . Among the immigrant groups, the Finns had an extra burden to carry. For a long time, the Finns were looked upon as Mongolians on the basis of a book written as long ago as 1775 by the German anthropologist J.F. Blumenbach, who had divided the world's people into five races based on color of skin. Since the Finns didn't fit easily into any of the five races, he lumped them in with the Mongols. Blumenbach's work had been the basis for all subsequent racial classifications and had been passed from one reference work to another, until anthropologists finally realized something was wrong.

The court case of the Finn, John Swan vs. the United States government, threatened to prevent any Finn from becoming an American citizen on the grounds that Finns were Mongolians, not "white persons" within the meaning of Section 2169, United States Revised Statutes. They were ineligible for citizenship based on a series of Oriental Exclusion Acts passed in 1882, 1892, 1902. On January 4, 1908, Swan and sixteen other Finns were denied citizenship by District Attorney John C. Sweet of St. Paul. However, on January 17 of that same year, Judge William A. Cant at the U.S. District Court, sitting in Duluth, officially declared that the Finns were not of the yellow race, that though perhaps the Finns had been "Mongols" in the remote past, their blood had been so tempered by that of the Teutonic and other races that they "are now among the whitest people in Europe." This relieved the Finns greatly, for they had adopted Western attitudes toward the yellow race. Reverberations from this controversy on Mongolianism were still in the air during my childhood. In fact, as late as 1957. . . the Knights and Ladies of Kaleva, a fraternal group of Finns, commissioned an amateur anthropologist to write a book "scientifically" disproving, once and for all, the theory that Finns are Asians. . . .

The Temperance Hall

The Clarence Ivonens, wearing folk dancing costumes, are shown in front of the 1906-07 Kaleva Hall in Virginia, Minnesota. Originally a Finnish Temperance Hall built in the early 1900s, the building served as a social, cutural, and ethnic entertainment center.

Some of the early Finnish immigrants had been young, unmarried men. Freed in this "new country" from the "old country" restraints of church, family, and community, they had begun to spend their free time in saloons, the one gathering place easily accessible to them. To woo the young men from these saloons, Finnish temperance societies, offering cultural and social activities and food, had been established

 The old dark Finnish Temperance Hall, which played such a great part in our family's life, is listed in the National Register of Historic Places and is known as Kaleva Hall. In 1968, the building was purchased by the Finnish Knights and Ladies of Kaleva, two cultural societies working together and made up primarily of people of Finnish backgrounds. The rituals of these two secret, benevolent orders and the names of their lodges are taken from the *Kalevala*, Finland's national epic.

THE SOCIALIST HALL

Courtesy of the Clatsop County Historical Society

The Socialist Hall in Astoria, Oregon, built in 1911, housed theatre, sports, sewing clubs, a store, and a workers' bureau.

EARLY TWENTIETH CENTURY
THE 1920S AND 30S — DEPRESSION YEARS
by Inkeri Väänänen-Jensen

In 1927, we bought our first car. . . . We never used our car in the winter months. In the late fall, the water was drained from the radiator. The battery was removed and hauled down into the basement; the car was put on blocks in the garage and forgotten until spring. Cars had no heaters so you bundled up in blankets if you were foolhardy enough to travel at all in cold weather. . . .

Like my father, most of the Finnish men on the Range worked in mining. In the open-pit mines, many Finns were day laborers who stripped away the overburden of glacial drift, rocks, pine needles, and soil in order to uncover the rich ore deposits lying underneath. . . . Many Finnish men also worked in underground mines, often under dangerous conditions.

Wages were low; many of the foreign-born mine employees earned between $10 and $15 per week for ten hours of labor each day, six days a week. From these wages, the cost of explosives, fuses, and caps were deducted, leaving even less in the pay envelope. . . . Many men were injured, maimed, or killed from falling rock, cave-ins, floods, misuse of explosives, or general carelessness, sometimes including drunkenness. A number of children on the North Side of Virginia had no fathers; they had been killed in mining accidents. . . .

On July 19, 1907, the miners on the Mesabi Range . . . asked the Oliver Mining Company for an eight-hour day, an end to bribes and bonuses, a day's wage of at least $2.50 for open-pit miners, and $3 for those working in dangerous underground mines. However, the Oliver refused; instead, it fired 300 miners, and brought in more than 1,000 strikebreakers, mostly Montenegrins and Croatians who had just arrived on the East Coast from the Old Country. They did not understand that they were strikebreakers. Some of them, when they realized that they were "scabs," quit their jobs. The strike lasted two months and at the end, many striking Finnish miners were blacklisted and barred from re-employment in the mines. Some went back to Finland, some moved to other states, others went to northern lumber camps, and many moved to farms in northeastern Minnesota. Nine years later the miners struck again . . . and lost again. Once more, many Finns moved to farms; others went to work in lumber camps; still others moved away from Minnesota. . . . Farm life, even on the poor cut-over, rocky land in northeastern Minnesota, seemed inviting when compared to the dangerous work in the mines. . . . These farms served as a safety valve for the blacklisted miners, allowing them to make a new start in America, even though eventually many of the farms proved to be unsuccessful economically. . . .

Family Affection

In our childhood, our family was not a demonstrative one. I never saw our mother and father kiss or hug each other. Their Finland backgrounds simply did not include these expressions of affection. I believe they looked upon kissing as an American custom. I have seen a short documentary on modern farm life in Finland in which the father had spent most of the winter months away from home working in the woods as a lumberjack. When he walked into the farmyard, his two children and his wife each greeted him with a handshake, but by their expressions one recognized that they were all extremely happy that he was home again. Nor did we children hug or kiss each other or our parents. We would have been embarrassed to do so. . . . Most of our experiences with various expressions of affection were vicarious, secondhand, that is, we saw them in the movies. . . . I do not recall kissing my parents until the time came for me to leave home for the university down in Minneapolis, and even then it was not an easy thing to do. But once the ice was broken, affectionate greetings and farewells no longer posed any problems. . . .

The Great Depression Hits
. . . But after the stock market crash of 1929, everything changed. The Great Depression began. . . . The Oliver Mining Company offered its miners work for five days each month at five dollars a day, giving us an income of twenty-five dollars a month. . . . it kept us from going hungry and also kept our father, plus many others, from being counted among the unemployed. . . .

We ate a lot of spaghetti, macaroni, bread, and hamburger, all of which we liked, for Lempi was a good cook and the food was tasty. We had a big garden. The cost of food was reasonable. One dollar bought a lot of groceries. A 1930 ad from a newspaper listed: "A large 12-quart basket of extra fancy, large Michigan Concord grapes, 33 cents . . . fancy light meat tuna fish, one-half pound cans, 2 for 25 cents. . . ." My brother Jorma tramped through the woods and shot an occasional rabbit, but we became concerned about tularemia, the rabbit disease, so we soon quit having wild rabbit on the menu. We ate a lot of fish that we caught in Vermilion and Burntside Lakes. We had a big garden, at first a plot provided by the school district. . . . Later we had a larger plot in the Oliver's large garden space for employees. . . . Our whole family worked in the garden. . . . I realize that one can get by with very little in terms of the physical comforts money can buy, but cannot get along without support from family, friends, and neighbors, and the organizations and institutions one belongs to. With such a network of support, one can manage even in difficult times. . . .

FAITHFUL HERITAGE: A THIRD-GENERATION FINNISH AMERICAN DISCOVERING FAMILY HERITAGE

by Joanne Asala

Joanne Asala is an author, editor, and adventure traveler based in Illinois. She has written more than thirty books on folklore, fairy tales, and ethnic topics, including Finnish-American Folklore: The Legend of St. Urho.

I grew up in the western suburbs of Chicago. In all my years of school, I think I knew only one other Finn kid, and he went by the name of Sihvonen. Like me, he was a third-generation Finnish American, isolated from a proper Finn community. What that means is that in eight years of primary school, and four of high school, no one knew how to pronounce my last name or could guess what ethnicity it was. "Asala? Is that Arabic or Turkish?" my teachers would ask. Or, "You don't look Asian with that blond hair, were you adopted?"

"No," I'd mumble, squirming in embarrassment at the scrutiny. Kids named Jones or Brown or Smith never had such trouble. "I'm Finnish."

"Finished? What are you finished with?" would be the usual reply. I'd force a smile and laugh along, like I hadn't heard that one a million times before!

Aside from a few Finnish cuss words that I learned from my great-grandmother Marta, and a few recipes that I was taught by older relatives, I really did not have much experience with Finnish culture in my younger years. When my great-grandparents came to the United States, it was important to learn English quickly and blend into the melting pot. Unlike today, many immigrants, by necessity or isolation, left their cultural traditions back in the Old World. Unless you were lucky enough to grow up on the Iron Range where many of your neighbors were also Finnish, customs quickly disappeared, and children born here grew up with an interest in and identity with American pop culture.

At times, my grandfather Edwin—a first-generation Finnish American—must have felt that his "Finnishness" was a burden. Back in the 1940s, he decided to shorten our surname from "Asiala" to "Asala." He was no doubt tired of explaining his heritage over and over again or correcting the pronunciation of his name, and hoped to simplify matters a bit with a briefer spelling.

It was not until I attended the first Asiala family reunion during my sophomore year of high school that I learned more about my heritage. There, for the first time, I was immersed in Finnish Pride, surrounded by more cousins and kinfolk than I ever knew I had. That first great gathering sparked a life-long interest in the foods, folklore, and traditions of Finland.

It was also at the reunion that I met my father's cousin Melvin Fennel (whose mother Stella was an Asiala), our official family historian. He put together a wonderful book of remembrance called *The Asiala Family: 500 Years in Finland and America*. It focuses on the arrival of my great-grandfather Karl Gustaf Asiala, who emigrated to the United States in 1889, and all of those who descended from Karl and his wife, Hilma Johanna Pollari. The book also traces our genealogy to an ancestor named Tapani Muhonen Asiainen, born in 1490—two years before Christopher Columbus sailed to America! It was the first time I had ever seen my family tree laid out on paper, and the feeling of seeing the names of all those ancestors is indescribable.

In his research, Melvin made a trip to Toholampi, Finland, the village where Great-Grandfather Karl was born. Melvin discovered that the family farm still exists on the very same plot of land it has occupied for centuries, and that the current residents are our cousins. He was able to re-establish ties between the branches of our family who had lost touch.

Melvin also discovered that the Asiala farm in Finland was one of the biggest in the region, and thus the inhabitants were forced to pay high taxes and took part in many business transactions. Contemporary documents frequently make mention of the Asiala farm and the people who lived on it, and because of all these factors, it was possible for him to trace our family tree much farther than the usual date of 1700, when the church began to keep official records. Melvin did not find any famous people or nobility in our family tree. But, as he says in the introduction of his book of remembrance, "I have proudly accepted the realization that my heritage is not hinged on the glory or notoriety of one person from the past, but stems from the proud traditions of an entire nation." I'll have to agree with him, for who we are today is formed, in part, by those who came before.

When I went to the university, I studied folklore and mythology and embarked on a quest to help preserve the Finnish-American culture which was in danger of becoming lost in many areas of the United States. I've been lucky to take part in a number of book projects that recorded these vanishing traditions, and at the same time educating myself about my own heritage—a heritage I'm still trying to piece together by working on our family tree.

The Internet has made this task much easier, with so many databases available at the click of a mouse. There aren't a large number of Asialas that came to the New World, and so it is not difficult to fit most of the names into our family tree. And the Internet has enabled me to contact distant cousins in Finland and all across the United States who are also studying the family tree. It is an exciting feeling to come across someone else's family tree on their Web page, and find members of your own lineage. By sharing information back and forth, you can end up with a family history that is more complete.

Of course, there are a few names in the genealogy databases that strike a note of curiosity. I found a Mateo Asala living in Bolivia in the 1700s, and an Anteo Asala in Mexico in the 1500s. Asala is not a Hispanic name. Can these men really be distant cousins—an Antti or a Matti Asiala—who made their way to the New World? Sons were always leaving the family farm when an older sibling inherited, maybe some sought their fortune on far distant shores. Only more research will eventually uncover the truth.

Because of the research begun by Melvin, there is a resurgent interest in Finnish customs in our family. My brother has picked a Finnish name for his son, and my father and I are planning a trip to Finland to see the old family farm for ourselves. I may be a third-generation Finnish American, but I still know who I am and where I came from.

Genealogical Resources

Much of our early family history came from information contained in the records of the Mormon Church in Salt Lake City, Utah. The church library, originally founded in 1894 to gather genealogical records of members of the Church of Jesus Christ of Latter-Day Saints, has a copy of nearly every genealogical record in the world. It is where most beginning genealogists start. With over 2.2 million rolls of microfilmed records, 742,000 microfiched records, 300,000 books, and 4,500 periodicals, it is the largest library of its kind in the world and open to the general public at no charge. Its International Genealogical Index database alone contains approximately 600 million individual names! The friendly and helpful staff is available for questions and consultations. For more information and hours of operation, contact the library at: Family History Library, 35 North West Temple Street, Salt Lake City, UT 84150-3400. Telephone (801) 240-2331. E-Mail: fhl@ldschurch.org. Or begin a preliminary search of your own at www.familyhistory.org. The web site has suggestions for conducting research in your particular state, as well as a general on-line search engine.

You may also wish to check out the new web site for the American Family Immigration History Center at www.ellisislandrecords.org. From 1892 to 1924, more than 22 million immigrants came through Ellis Island the Port of New York. You may find your ancestor on the manifests, the lists of passengers, the shipping companies kept. The center also sells photographs of some of these ships, and copies of the original manifests— perfect to hang beside a photo of your ancestor! Although I have not managed to find my great-grandfather in this database, I have found several other Asialas who came from the same small village in Finland, and who are, no doubt, related.

OTHER SOURCES

Ancestry.com (www.ancestry.com) bills itself as the leader in on-line family history, and offers over one billion names in its databases, with new records added daily. It charges a fee for its services, but also offers a trial membership.

RootsWeb.com (www.rootsweb.com) is a free on-line site which provides interactive guides and research tools for tracing your family tree. Their WorldConnect Project has 73 million names and counting.

Additional Sites for Finnish-American Genealogical Research

From Marian Eliason, University of Minnesota, Minneapolis

www.genealogia.fi
The Genealogical Society of Finland. From this site you can search HisKi (Finnish parish records online). Join the Finngen mailing list; search Finngen archives; connect with Finnish, North American, and other researchers, and find more information about Finnish and Finnish-American genealogy than you ever imagined.

www.utu.fi/erill/instmigr/index_e.htm
Institute of Migration in Turku, Finland. On-line search for Finnish passports and ship passenger records. The institute promotes migration research, conducts and publishes studies and books, and fosters cooperation between organizations within Finland and abroad for the purpose of studying Finnish migration.

www1.umn.edu/ihrc/
Immigration History Research Center, University of Minnesota, has an exceptionally rich collection of Finnish and Finnish-American archival materials, including microfilmed Finnish-language, Finnish-American newspapers, and the family histories compiled for the 1980 Finnish-American Family History Project.

www.finlandia.edu/06a.html (from Jim Kurtti)
The Finnish American Heritage Center in Hancock, Michigan, has one of the most significant collections of Finnish-American genealogical materials—not only from Finnish-American sources, but also filmed church records from Finland—covering all the areas of major immigration. It also has a large collection of personal genealogies and biographies as well as family, community, and regional histories from Finland and the entire range of the publications produced by the Finnish Genealogical Society in Finland.

FINNISH CANADIANS

By the year 2000, just under 100,000 people of Finnish heritage were living in Canada, where early immigrants found similar land formations and the familiar birch trees. The first Finnish settlement was New Finland, located west of the Manitoba border on the banks of the Qu'Appelle Valley, north of Wapella and Whitewood, Saskatchewan. Author-artist Hazel Lauttamus Birt grew up in New Finland, and records the life of these early Northwest Territory homesteaders in her book, *The Finns of New Finland, 1888–1993*. By 1900 all the free land in the wooded area of the valley was gone, but settlers continued to arrive. They found abandoned homesteads or were able to purchase land at a modest price. Many continued westward where free land on the prairie was still available.

Life was hard in the new territory, but by its "hey-day," the community of New Finland numbered 700 Finns. As the community grew, they had their schools, church, community hall, library, blacksmiths, tanners, weavers, builders, mid-wives, and barbers. Today, most of the small farms have become a part of large spreads. Some still farm small holdings, and some original homesteads have been preserved as summer homes, but services and social life have expanded to surrounding communities.

Finnish immigrants continued to come to Canada. Many came seeking better opportunities and relief from political tensions in three main migration periods: from the 1880s to World War I, many were recruited by the railway and were attracted by the boom of industrialization in Canada; the second wave, 1919–1930, followed the civil war in Finland, when many were discontent with the ruling regime; the 1947–1967 period included many of the Eastern Finns who were dislocated by the Soviet annexation of Karelia. Their enterprise and hard work helped to open up parts of Canada. A strong concern for social justice contributed to the democratic process, especially through the labor movements, mutual aid and cooperation, and women's rights.

Senior centers in Vancouver, Thunder Bay, Sault Ste. Marie, Timmins, Sudbury, and Toronto are centers of community activity. The Finnish language is taught at summer camps and through the famous Ontario International Languages Program. The University of Toronto offers a comprehensive Finnish Studies program, as well as publishes the *Journal of Finnish Studies*. The Finnish language is also taught at Lakehead University.

Many Finnish Canadians have caught the attention of a broader society in the areas of business, education, and physical fitness. Among these are: Peter Nygård, well-known clothing designer; Jukka-Pekka Sarasate, conductor of the Toronto Symphony Orchestra; Paul Siren, an influential leader of the UAW during World War II who received an Order of Canada honor; and Teemu Selänne and Saku Koivu, celebrated hockey players. The Canadian National Olympic Teams often include Finnish Canadians.

The National Archives of Canada, 395 Wellington Street, Ottawa, Ontario, I1A ON3, is a rich resource of records documenting the Finnish-Canadian community. Scholarly works on Finnish life and translations of Finnish literature are an important part of the University of Toronto's Finnish Studies program; notably among these is the work of Börje Vähämäki, historian, translator, and founding editor of the *Journal of Finnish Studies,* and his wife, Varpu Lindström, author and professor at York University.

North American writers attending a seminar at the University of Toronto in 2000 included Burt Rairamo; Richard Impola; Professor K. Börje Vähämäki, publisher of Aspasia Books; Ernest Hekkanen; Karen Driscoll; Harri Siitonen; and Mary Caraker.

PLACES, PEOPLE, EVENTS
Where the Finns Are

More than 700,000 Americans are of Finnish ancestry. Nearly half of them live in the North Central region, from Minnesota to Ohio. Michigan, Minnesota, and Wisconsin have more than one-third of the total. California, Washington, Florida, and Massachusetts also have large Finnish populations.

On the Delaware

The first Finnish settlers to cross the Atlantic landed in 1638 on the Delaware River at the present site of Wilmington, Delaware. Finnish know-how went into the first log cabins built here. Churches, homes, and forts were built of logs. The colony of New Sweden included parts of the present states of Delaware, New Jersey, and Pennsylvania. A marker erected by the Pennsylvania Historical and Museum Commission proclaims: "Finland: The name given to a tract along the Delaware River from Marcus Hook to Chester River. Grant for tract was given Captain Hans Amundsson Besk, a native of Finland, by Queen Christina in 1653. Site of first Finnish settlement in America."

John Morton
Finnish-American Descendant Casts Decisive Vote for United States Declaration of Independence

The date was July 2, 1776. The Continental Congress was meeting in Philadelphia to vote on the resolution, "Should the thirteen colonies sever all ties to Great Britain?" A unanimous vote for independence was needed. Only the delegates from Pennsylvania were split on the negative side; the outcome of the vote was dependent upon Pennsylvania delegate John Morton. When Morton voted "Aye!" the United States was born.

John Morton's great-grandfather had emigrated from Finland to New Sweden in 1654. Records indicate that Morton's ancestors (Marttinen) were from the parish of Rautalampi in Savo. These early pioneers in the Delaware colony were most likely among those driven from their home-steads in Sweden due to the Swedish king's forest conservation policies

John Morton, (1724–1777) whose great-grandfather was born in Rautalampi, Finland, signed the Declaration of Independence in 1776 with Benjamin Franklin, John Hancock, Thomas Jefferson, John Adams, and fifty-one other patriots.

Library of Congress photograph

Photograph from Kay and Richard Atkinson

Morton Homestead
Governor Printz Park
Prospect Park, Pennsylvania
One of the oldest structures in the state, the building was constructed in the mid-seventeenth century of logs hewn by Morton Mårtensson, Finnish great-grandfather of John Morton.

restricting "cut and burn" methods of land cultivation. John Morton's grandfather was eight years old when he arrived in the New World. Morton died a few months after signing the Declaration of Independence.

Massachusetts Finns

One of the most active communities preserving the Finnish heritage is Fitchburg, Massachusetts, home of Fitchburg State College, which opened its Finnish Cultural Center in 1964 to promote and preserve Finnish culture and heritage. The Finnish Labor Society, *Saima,* founded in 1894, supported American labor movements and Finnish cultural activities for many years. Finnish immigrants, looking for a brighter future, settled in Fitchburg in the late 1800s. Some services are held in the Finnish language at two churches—the Messiah Lutheran Church, founded in 1893, and the Elm Street Congregational Church, founded in 1898.

The Fitchburg group created beautiful Saima Park on the site of a rundown farm, where the New England Finnish Summer Festival is held each year. Featuring a bonfire, dancing, musical performances, sporting events, art exhibits, a Finnish coffee-bread contest, serious socializing, and distinguished speakers, festival proceeds benefit a leading Finnish-language newspaper, *Raivaaja,* which was published daily for fifty years, beginning in 1905, but is now a weekly and includes a section in English.

Maine Finns

The emigration of Finns to the State of Maine was concentrated within three regions. The earliest was in the mid-coastal area, encompassing the three small counties of Knox, Lincoln, and Waldo. A second region was in Oxford County, nearly 100 miles inland to the northwest. The third area was in the Piscataquis County town of Monson, located approximately 100 miles north of the "mid-coast" and the same distance to the east from Oxford County. These settlers were first attracted by the jobs available in the mid-coast granite quarries, and the slate quarries in Monson. Lumbering jobs were available in Oxford County. The ultimate goal was the purchase of small farms within those areas.

Each of these regions still contain descendants of these early immigrants, and each has a Finnish-American organization of its own. A Finnish Congregational Church is still active in the coastal town of South Thomaston, and it is the only remaining Finnish church of this denomination in North America. The popular national FinnFest was held in Gorham, Maine in 1998, with the "10th Annual Finn Funn Weekend" scheduled for the Samoset Resort in Rockport on October 2002.

—Art Jura

Florida Finns

Palm Beach County records the largest Finnish-American community outside Europe. About 30,000 Finns who like warm weather call Florida home, living in Lake Worth and Lantana, adjacent cities on the Atlantic coast about fifty miles north of Miami. Most members of the Finnish community are year-round residents. Several thousand others spend winters in Florida and summers in northern United States and Canada. Several thousand more come each winter from Finland.

A Finnish Consulate office is located in Lake Worth. Lantana-Lake Worth is one of ten U.S. locations for voting in Finnish elections. A Finnish

Business Chamber of Commerce was formed in 1975, with more than 150 businesses owned by Finns—twenty-five of them construction firms. Former chamber president Alfons Ukkonen said, "They built practically all of Lantana."

An annual "Finlandia" festival has been held in Lake Worth since 1985. Finnish Independence Day, December 6, is observed with commemorative services and celebrations at the area's two Finnish community

Lantana and Lake Worth, Florida, both promote cultural exchanges with sister cities in Finland. Lapua in Finland's Vaasa Province is a sister city to Lantana. Lappeenranta, located east of the Russian border, is Lake Worth's counterpart. Editor's Note: Fitchburg, Massachusetts, and Kokkola, Finland, have been sister cities since 1972. Cultural exchange programs between the cities have taken place.

Ohio Finns

Between the mid-1860s and the 1930s, more than 4,000 Finns lived in Ohio. The largest settlement was the Ashtabula area. The earliest immigrants came to lay track for the railroad in 1872, but when that work was finished they moved on to wherever work led them. The first permanent settlers came a few years later to do the back-breaking work of shoveling iron ore from ships' holds onto the railroad cars on the docks. They lived in an area which eventually became known as "Finn Town." The first Finnish church was the Finnish Congregational Church (eventually it joined the Suomi Synod of the Finnish Evangelical Lutheran Church) in Ashtabula Harbor. It was destroyed by fire in 1891, and was subsequently rebuilt. The churches played an important role in the lives of early Finnish Americans, but the early temperance unions were the places where families found their niche in a new nation. Various temperance unions succeeded or failed depending on the effort of the membership. A merger in 1910 created a single temperance society, but following World War II, only the five founding members remained faithful. The building was eventually demolished, and in its place is a park owned by the Ashtabula Area Museum and Historical Society, gifted by Captain Victor Anderson, a local Finnish-American Great Lakes ship pilot, as an asset of the Ashtabula County Finnish-American Heritage Association.

Old World Wisconsin

Eagle, Wisconsin

A large outdoor museum has more than forty buildings originally constructed by immigrant settlers. Two of the eight farmsteads are Finnish, with seven buildings from 1910–1920. The restored buildings are in the midst of fields of grain, kitchen gardens, and fenced pastures. Guides and costumed staff members explain the historical context of this living museum. The site is open May through October.

Vieno Keskimaki stands in front of the Ketola house. She is wearing what the lady of the house, Maria Ketola, might have worn in 1915. The house was built between 1894 and 1900 in Oulu, Bayfield County, Wisconsin. It is an excellent example of Finnish log construction with dovetail corner notching.

Gerry Kangas photograph

Old Brule, Wisconsin
Heritage Society Grist Mill

The historic Davidson windpowered grist mill in Old Brule, listed on the National Register of Historic Places, was donated to the Heritage Society by Bill and Gene Davidson, son and grandson of Jacob Tapiola (changed to Davidson), Finnish immigrant who built the mill, which could grind up to 300 pounds of grain an hour in the early 1900s. The Heritage Society hopes to create an interpretive center with a display of early farm history.

Markham, Minnesota

Eli Wirtanen Finnish Farmstead

This farmstead, owned by a nonprofit group called Friends of the Wirtanen Pioneer Farm, has been a tourist attraction since 1974 with twenty-five cleared acres in the midst of forty acres. Eli Wirtanen homesteaded the land in 1904 and built everything on the farm. The sixteen buildings include a bathhouse, woodshed, guest house, residence, well-house, log horse barn, hay shed, root cellar, outhouse, log woodshed, shingle mill, pig pen, barn, and shelter to cover the old surrey.

Esko, Minnesota

Palkie Grist Mill Museum

The Historical Society of Esko (Minnesota) has created the Palkie Grist Mill Museum including an 1878 grist mill, an 1885 granary, and an 1897 one-room schoolhouse, used by Finnish immigrants in northeastern Minnesota.

Kitchen artifacts at Esko

New York Mills, Minnesota
Finn Creek Open-Air Museum

The Finnish-American Historical Society of New York Mills purchased 9.7 acres of the pioneer Finnish farmstead of Siffert and Wilhelmiina Tapio and began restoration of the buildings. At the beginning, only a house and sauna were on the place. Buildings now include a summer kitchen and granary. A fence of the style once used in Finland has been placed around the acreage. Beginning in the late 1970s, the Finn Creek Farmstead has been the site of handcraft fairs and folk music festivals.

Cokato, Minnesota

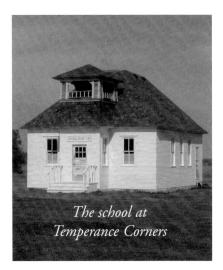

The Cokato Finnish-American Historical Society was chartered in 1938 as an extension of the 300th anniversary celebration of the first Finnish settlement in Delaware. The society maintains the Historic Temperance Hall, log cabin, schoolhouse and smoke sauna located at Temperance Corners (just north of Cokato). Annual events include a fall festival in early October and the Memorial Day Celebration the Saturday before Memorial Day.

The school at Temperance Corners

Embarrass, Minnesota

Finnish Pioneer Homesteads

Located approximately ninety miles north of Duluth on Minnesota's Mesabi Iron Range, Embarrass is rich in Finnish heritage. Naming of this community in the early 1700s is attributed to a French cleric, Father Du Poisson, who described the word meaning obstacles of logs, etc., in and about the waterways. Finnish woodsmen followed, with their axes, picks, and determination *(sisu)*.

They carved out their new homes, tilled the fields, and turned Indian paths into roads. The community was nearly 100 percent Finnish until the taconite mines attracted a melting pot of nationalities in the 1950s. A Finnish-American Summer Festival is held in June. Tours of Finnish Pioneer Homesteads run from Memorial Day through Labor Day. Sisu Heritage Inc., a community promotion group, works to preserve historic Finnish landmarks.

Farmer's Wife and Miner
Carved wooden statues at Embarrass, Minnesota

Photos courtesy the Embarrass Finnish Pioneer Homestead

Chisholm, Minnesota

The Iron Range Discovery Center

Iron ore was discovered on Gunflint Lake in 1849. This find raised speculation that gold as well might be explored, creating a trail to Duluth and other sources of Minnesota's mineral wealth. Gold was not found, but mining and lumbering flourished, initiating the founding of the towns of Tower, Soudan, Ely, Mountain Iron, Hibbing, and Virginia. The effects of the boom and bust of large industry were felt strongly by the workers who migrated to these areas. In many of the community Finn Halls, the movement for better working conditions began.

In the 1980s, with an economic recession throughout the country, many left the range, going to the Twin Cities, California, Arizona, Texas, Colorado, and Florida. The population that was lost has not been restored. The Ironworld Discovery Center at Chisholm, Minnesota, open to the public year-round, preserves and disseminates this Iron Range history, as well as provides a source for genealogical research.

This Finnish kick-sled was once owned by Mrs. Victor Juselin of Brimson, Minnesota, who hauled her groceries with it. The sled toured in the 1980s with the "Circles of Tradition" tour, sponsored by the University of Minnesota. Gerry Kangas loaned the sled to the Loon Lake Museum, in Palo, Minnesota.

Copper Country Michigan Finns

Keweenaw Peninsula

In 1843, early adventurers sailed into a small harbor in the Northwest Territories at the upper tip of Michigan, the Keweenaw Peninsula. News of copper finds and new mines up and down the peninsula marked the beginning of European settlements. A majority of early Finns came not from Finland, but from northern Norway where they had emigrated during periods of famine; there was also a significant number of Samis, Norwegians, and Swedes. Earliest settlements are Houghton, Calumet, and Hancock. An annual mid-winter's day celebration, *Heikinpäivä*, with parade, activities, and market is held at Hancock in January.

Kaleva, Michigan

In this community where one-fourth of the residents are Finnish, the tradition of lighting candles in the cemetery copies a similar tradition in Finland at Christmas time. The cemetery has several acres with twinkling lights on the graves of all, not just the Finnish dead.

Michigan's Finnish Cultural Center

Farmington Hills, Michigan

The cultural center provides activities for more than 1,700 families of the Finnish Center Association, founded in 1966. The cultural center, built in 1974, has a large auditorium, well-equipped kitchen, import store, members' lounge, library, and offices.

Baraga County, Michigan

Finnish Homestead Museum

Near Hancock, the Finnish Homestead Museum farmhouse is kept as it was in the 1920s. It is typical of the farmhouses built by early immigrants who brought their customs and ways with them.

Bloomfield Hills, Michigan

Cranbrook Academy of Art

Located twenty-five miles northwest of Detroit, the Cranbrook Academy of Art is the largest artifact representing the work of Finnish-born architect Eliel Saarinen. The structures on this 300-acre campus reflect the changing course of architecture in the first half of the twentieth century, when Saarinen designed and became the first president of the academy. Cranbrook's wealth of decorative detail in iron, brick, stone and tile, wood and bronze, glass and concrete make it one of the finest examples of total design in America. The collaboration between the founders of the academy, George Gough Booth and Ellen Scripps Booth, along with Saarinen produced this National Historic Landmark. The Saarinen family influence is reflected in furnishings, textiles, and overall architectural design. The Cranbrook Educational Community, which includes Cranbrook Academy of Art and Museum, Cranbrook Institute of Science, and Cranbrook Schools, is open to visitors year-round.

Hancock, Michigan

Finlandia University

Finnish immigrants dreamed of an institution that would provide religious education, perpetuate the Finnish language, and preserve their experience in North America. Members of the Finnish Evangelical Lutheran Church founded Suomi College, now Finlandia University, in 1896. Today the Hancock, Michigan, university serves some 400 students from many backgrounds, including third- and fourth-generation Finns. It became affiliated with the Evangelical Lutheran Church in America in 1988, but offers nonsectarian instruction, counseling, and worship services.

Currently under the leadership of President Robert A. Ubbelohde, the university is made up of two colleges and two schools: the Suomi College of Arts & Sciences, the College of Professional Studies, the International School of Art & Design, and the International School of Business. Situated in the beautifully rugged peninsula landscape, some campus buildings reflect Finnish heritage: the Finnish American Heritage Center, Paavo Nurmi Athletic Center, Nikander Hall (named after J.K. Nikander, first president), Finlandia Hall, Mannerheim Hall, Wargelin Hall, Kivi House, and Sulo and Aileen Maki Library.

The Finnish American Heritage Center, Finlandia University

Finlandia University's Finnish American Heritage Center, directed by Jim Kurtti, links the Finnish-American community by history, tradition, and mission, to Finland. Remodeled from a Catholic church built in 1885, the Heritage Center features the original vaulted tin ceiling and houses a theater, art gallery, museum, and the Finnish-American Historical Archives (FAHA). The Heritage Center continues to be a community focal point by offering traveling exhibits, lectures, plays, and musical programs linking the Finnish-American community to Finland.

The FAHA has the distinction of housing the most comprehensive Finnish-American archival collection in the world. More than 20,000 items are carefully preserved within the climate-controlled archival stacks. The archives were established in 1932. The mission of the FAHA is to collect and preserve the multi-faceted history of North American Finns. In addition, the archives have a significant collection of materials from Canada, Finland, and other countries. Patrons are encouraged to make donations of Finnish-American materials to the FAHA.

Art enthusiasts enjoy the ever-changing exhibits found in the Center Gallery. The Center Theater offers a variety of programs. Members of the Heritage Center Society assist in the preservation of Finnish-American culture. Support of patrons, financial and otherwise, is vital to the continuation of Finnish-American identity.

Exterior of the Finnish American Heritage Center Hancock, Michigan

North Dakota

Nearly 4,000 people of Finnish background live in North Dakota, especially in the Brocket, Lakota, and Pelto areas in the east central area of the state.

West Coast Finns

The California gold rush of 1849 lured the first Finns to California. By 1858, families were arriving and community and social activities were being established. Montana, Washington, and Oregon also have large Finnish-American populations.

A number of Finnish-American engineers and architects contributed to building the cities of the western United States, including Seattle and Portland. One was A.W. Quist, born in Finland, who studied with Eliel Saarinen. He formed his own construction company, and in the 1920s and 1930s built nearly 200 structures in Washington state, Alaska, Oregon, and Hawaii. Finnish-born Alpo J. "Al" Tokola, engineer, helped build the world's highest arch bridge, the Glen Canyon Bridge, 645 feet above the Colorado River, and the Fremont Bridge, the world's largest tied-arch span, 1,255 feet across the Willamette River in Portland, Oregon.

There are large settlements of Finnish Americans in the Deep River area of Washington and in Astoria, Oregon.

San Diego, California
House of Finland

The House of Finland is one of approximately thirty ethnic cottages at Balboa Park in San Diego, California. The cottages are part of the House of Pacific Relations, run by the U.S. Government. During the winter of 1939, the American Red Cross asked San Diego Finns to help their native Finland. Finnish Americans banded together and formed the House of Finland, a nonprofit organization, and became a part of the Balboa Park group. The cottages are open to the public on Sundays. There is an annual festival held on the lawn with folk dancers, singers, and Finnish foods, attracting thousands of visitors.

Pasadena, California

Finnish Folk Art Museum

A replica of a Finnish home *(tupa)* has been erected on the grounds of the Feynes Mansion in Pasadena. Once the home of the Finnish Consul, Y.A. Paloheimo, the building houses an impressive array of antiquities from Finland, many of which are on display. The *tupa,* in olden times, was a multi-purpose room combining functions of a kitchen, dining room, living room, and even bedroom. Most of the furnishings in this *tupa* are from the province of Ostrobothnia, Pohjanmaa, in Northwestern Finland. The museum is open to visitors.

Oregon Finns

A 1880 Clatsop County census lists fourteen Finnish women and 189 Finnish men; 171 of the men were fishermen. The opening of fish canneries along the Columbia River increased the demand for skilled fishermen. This attracted many Finnish immigrants.

In 1896 The Union Fisherman's Cooperative Packing Company was established in Astoria, with Finns being the largest ethnic group among its founders and charter members, who brought the spirit of the cooperative movement they saw taking hold in Europe. The structure of the cannery benefited both the industry of the canneries and the fishermen. The building and dock area have been dismantled, but the Uniontown area in the west part of Astoria, where most of the early Finnish population lived, still has sites and relics of this past.

The Clatsop County Historical Museum, operates four buildings in Astoria: the Flavel House with associated Carriage House, dating to about 1886; the Uppertown Fire Museum, and the Heritage Museum. They depict the pioneer spirit of an earlier era. Other points of interest are the Columbia River Maritime Museum, the Fort Astoria site and the newly restored Liberty Theatre. The Erik Lindgren Log Cabin Museum at Cullaby Lake Park, between Gearhart and Astoria in Clatsop County, was dismantled and moved from Soapstone Valley to its present location. Built originally by two Finns, Erik Lindgren and William Merila, using only primitive tools, the house is maintained by the Finnish-American Historical Society of the West, and is open on weekends during the summer.

Seattle, Washington

Nordic Heritage Museum

Finnish artifacts on display at the Nordic Heritage Museum in Seattle, Washington, include a fine example of the Finnish musical instrument, the kantele, and a handpainted stage curtain from the old Finnish Brotherhood Hall of Seattle, dated 1912.

Celebrations sponsored by the museum include the Tivoli Festival in July and the Yulfest in November. Finnish groups set up booths and demonstrate traditional music and folk dancing. Regular programs at the museum feature weaving, rosemaling, woodcarving, folk music, dance, language instruction, and an annual crafts fair to preserve the heritage of Finland, Norway, Sweden, Denmark, and Iceland. The museum is housed in a former school building in Seattle.

Seattlen Suomi Koulu—Finnish School of Seattle

The Finnish language is taught at this school housed in the Seattle Finnish Lutheran Church. The church is built in the Finnish tradition with a wooden interior. A center for the Seattle-area Finnish-American community, many cultural events and meetings are held here.

Deep River area, Washington

There are many Finnish Americans in this area.

Finns in Alaska

Finns were among the earliest settlers of Alaska and the Pacific Coast as far south as California. After 1809, the year Russia was given control of Finland by treaty, Finns were aboard the Russian vessels that sailed around the Cape of Good Hope and all the way back to Alaska. Finns were among those who stayed. Two Finns became governors of Alaska. They were Arvid Adolph Etholen and Hampus Furuhjelm. The first white child born at the Alaska Railroad construction camp, later the site of the city of Anchorage, was born to Finnish parents; Leo Saarela grew up to become a mining engineer and a Territorial Commissioner of Mines. The Anchorage Suomi-Finland Club, established in 1920 as a social and cultural program, is one of the oldest fraternal-social organizations in Alaska.

Nurturing Finnish Roots

International, national, and regional groups for North American Finns promote cultural exchanges and heritage preservation. Almost immediately upon settlement in an area, the immigrants joined together in churches, temperance, and socialist halls, forging ties to each other and to their homeland. They founded drama groups, benevolent societies, and other societies for the preservation and protection of their heritage.

Today there are Finnish studies programs at several institutions in the United States and Canada including Finlandia University and the universities of Toronto, Minnesota, and Washington.

Typical of the cultural groups is the Yrjö Kilpinen Society of North America, Ltd., which held the first international Yrjö Kilpinen symposium and art song competition at Edgewood College in Madison, Wisconsin, in 1999, to promote the composer's songs. He has composed more than 800 songs to poems written in Finnish, Swedish, and German including works from the *Kalevala* and *Kanteletar*.

Dozens of historical societies and cultural organizations exist from Maine and Connecticut to Alaska, and there are many genealogy groups. Only a few of the many organizations are noted here. More complete information of all things Finnish can be found on the worldwide web.

The Knights and Ladies of Kaleva

Founded over a century ago by John Stone, this Finnish fraternal organization is dedicated to the preservation of Finnish heritage in the United States and Canada. The first Kaleva Lodge was organized in 1898 in Belt, Montana. Along with personal values and interest in all things Finnish, these groups work toward brotherly love within and outside their fraternity.

Finland Society

Founded in 1927 and headquartered in Helsinki, the society provides a cultural bridge for some 200,000 member Finns and their descendants worldwide.

Finn-Spark, Inc.

Established in 1949 by a group of women of Finnish descent, whose spouses were in the Washington, D.C., area on government or business assignments, for the purpose of maintaining the Finnish language among its members, to encourage Finnish culture and traditions, and to make Finland better known, this group has expanded to include second-generation Americans. They actively support various Finnish and Finnish-American charitable causes.

Project 34

With an emphasis on long-range strategies for perpetuating Finnish culture in America, this structured effort is most visible in the form of an annual conference where lectures and discussions provide both informative and practical approaches for education and activities. They also provide an Internet service, posting many activities of Finnish interest.

Finlandia Foundation

This nonprofit American organization is dedicated to Finnish culture and Finnish-American exchange. Established in 1953, it is the most important private source of support for Finnish culture in the United States today. The Foundation has twenty-two chapters nationwide, and approximately 3,000 members. Each chapter sponsors its own cultural events and several award scholarships. The Finlandia Foundation Trust has given approximately $100,000 per year in grants and scholarships for the past several years. Detailed information about the Finlandia Foundation and its chapters may be found on the Internet.

The Swedish-Finn Historical Society

Founded in 1991, this group seeks to preserve the role and history of Swedish-speaking Finnish immigrants from western and southern Finland who settled in seventeen regions of the United States and Canada. Swedish-Finns included: General C.G.E. Mannerheim, John Morton, Johan Ludvig Runeberg, composer Jean Sibelius, and historian Dr. Anders M. Myhrman, who wrote about the Swedish-Finns in America.

Documenting this history, Syrene and Don Foresman point out that the Swedish and Finnish colonists in the Delaware New Sweden Colony (1638) not only contributed log cabin building techniques but also introduced planting rye in the ashes of burned forest logs, multi-harness weaving of linen and woolen coverlets, and cleared forests along the Delaware River. It is noted that William Penn purchased large estates from the New Sweden colonists to complete the state of Pennsylvania.

FinnFest USA

An event attracting from five to eight thousand people interested in their Finnish-American culture, FinnFest USA is held annually. Beginning in 1983, the event has been held in Maine, California, Delaware, Washington, Florida, Illinois, Oregon, Massachusetts, three times in Michigan, and twice in Minnesota with a third celebration scheduled for 2002 in Minneapolis with the theme "Under the North Star" *("Pohjantähden Alla')*.

It all began when thirty-nine Finnish-American organizations met with Tauri Aaltio, executive director of the Finland Society of Helsinki. In a contest to name the American event, Sirkka Wilson of Seattle won with FinnFest USA. The late Robert W. Selvala became the first president with Velma Doby, secretary, and Lois M. Nelson, treasurer.

Bert Kivimaki of Toronto has noted that for over forty years the Finnish Canadian Cultural Federation has hosted an annual festival. In the year 2000, FinnFest USA was held in Toronto jointly with the federation.

Five days and nights of cultural events and fun are planned for the 2002 Fest in Minneapolis. Over seventy musical events are planned, highlighted by the release of a new hymn book thanks to Paul Niemisto of St. Olaf College, Gracie Grindahl of Luther Seminary, and Marianne Wargelin, Honorary Finnish Consul, and others, supported by a Finlandia Foundation Trust Grant. Prof. Richard Impola summarized the spirit of FinnFest USA in the *Upper Peninsula Post* in 1995. He views FinnFest as a transfer to the national level of old Finn-Hall or church and cultural activities. The halls were once the center in the Finnish-American community for social, cultural, and entertainment purposes, with dances, plays, choral concerts, speeches, and poetry recitals. Nearly all had theatrical groups, a chorus or two, an athletic club, and maybe an orchestra or band. Among the nationally known performers in musicals was Rosa Lemberg, born in Namibia to an Arabian-African mother and English father, educated in a Finnish mission school in Africa and in Finland. In America, she became a performer in Finnish-American theatre.

Professor Impola makes the point that the Finns seem to hold on to their language longer than other immigrants, perhaps because it differs more from English than other European languages. Carl Pellonpaa tells of his father, who refused to speak English except for two words: If the phone rang and he was home alone he answered, "Nobody home!" and hung up.

Special Foods of the Finns

by Inkeri Väänänen-Jensen

Most Finnish homes always had on hand "something for coffee," most often a cardamon-flavored, sweet, yeast bread called *pulla* in Finland but Finnish biscuit on the Iron Range. A slice of buttered fresh Finnish biscuit was especially favored with a freshly brewed cup of "egg" coffee, in which an egg was mixed with the coffee, preferably newly ground in a hand-operated grinder. This mixture was spooned into boiling water in the coffee pot on the stove, boiled for a few minutes, and then set aside to settle before it was served. Coffee visitors often were also served *korppuja*, which were either homemade rusks baked with a butter, sugar, and cinnamon topping, or store-bought zwieback. Or they could be served open-face cheese, egg salad, or cold meat sandwiches, homemade cookies, doughnuts, or cake. Always "prepared," we welcomed coffee company at any time. After I was married, it took years before I accepted that it was all right to serve guests just coffee and nothing else. For years, I was always "prepared."

At home our daily bread was a homemade crusty whole-wheat bread baked in a pie tin as a *limppu* (round loaf). We also usually had on hand a heavy, thick, brown hardtack made from rye flour and purchased either from the Finnish bakery or the Finnish co-op store in twelve-inch "wheels," each with a hole in the center. Our parents enjoyed it, but we children left it pretty much alone in the early years. It was too thick, too hard, and too sour for our tastes. The term now often used for this hardtack is "crisp bread," much of it imported from the Nordic countries, Finland included. To go with the hardtack, our mother made bowls of what was called either *viiliä* or *fiiliä* (Finnish yogurt), depending on what part of Finland your parents came from. It was thick, soured whole milk with a wrinkled yellow cream top, kept cool in the icebox. During the summers, it was a refreshing mainstay of the noon meal. We often sprinkled sugar over the rich, creamy top.

A particularly popular supper was pea soup cooked with a ham bone, with oven-baked pancake for dessert. The oven pancake, mostly eggs, milk, and flour baked in a large pan and then sprinkled with sugar, was especially palatable and popular. Once in a while when a farm friend's cow or pig was butchered, we would have *verilättyjä* (blood pancakes). They were delicious, dark and crisp at the edges. Our parents enjoyed them, but the thought of what they were made of turned us children against them. Blood pancakes eventually became the rarest of treats. Our farm friends also brought what was known as *uunijuusto* (oven cheese), but we called it farmer cheese. It was made with the first milk from a cow that had just had a calf. The cheese was in the form of a thick, round pancake browned in the oven. It squeaked and was rubbery. We liked it. You can still buy squeaky cheese in some grocery stores in the Copper Country.

Our regular pancakes were always made "from scratch" and were thin and large. In the early days, we ate them with butter and white sugar. Only later did we learn to use syrup, which our mother made of brown sugar, water, and maple flavoring. . . .

Another great favorite of the Finns was the Cousin Jack pasty borrowed from the Cornish miners known as Cousin Jacks who frequently carried pasties in their lunch pails. The wives of the Cornish miners baked chunks of flank steak (then an economy cut) in a pie-type crust folded into a half-moon shape over potatoes and onions— easy to eat as a hand-pie and good either hot or cold. From the Old Country, many Finns were used to *piirakkas* (derived from Russian *pierogis*), a crust usually filled with rice or potatoes, so for the Finnish immigrant housewife it was an easy and natural step to the Cousin Jack pasty. It became a favorite on Finnish tables and in Finnish lunch pails. Nowadays, less expensive cuts of beef or even ground beef are used, and some pork, carrots, turnips, or rutabagas may be added. A number of Iron Range bakeries sell pasties, a regional delicacy. . . .

When Finnish groups such as a church congregation or a temperance society held summer outings at nearby lakes, the special dish was mojakka, most often a soup made with freshly caught fish, milk, potatoes, onions, and black peppercorns, or it could be a rich garden-fresh vegetable and beef soup. We always thought mojakka was a special name brought from Finland, but discovered that the word was unknown there until it was brought to Finland by American Finns.

One of our frequent and favorite meat dishes was what we called *lihapullia* (meatballs). Round, small, well-browned with chopped onions and a smattering of allspice, the meatballs were served in their own brown gravy over boiled or mashed potatoes. Another ground beef favorite was *kaalikääryjä* (cabbage rolls). Ground beef and rice, with allspice as the flavoring, were wrapped in cabbage leaves made soft and pliable through steaming. These were baked in the oven for a long time and were often served with baked potatoes.

A special vegetable prepared on holidays was *lanttulaatikko* (rutabaga casserole). Cooked and mashed rutabagas were mixed with eggs, cream, butter, and nutmeg and then baked. In the early years we had few salads, but our mother did make one as the main part of a meal, *punajuurikkasalaatti* (beet salad). We children did not care for it, but would try to eat a little. It consisted of cut-up cooked beets, diced onions, salted herring, boiled and chopped eggs, and diced apple with a dressing.

At Christmastime our parents' great delight came on Christmas Eve. After we had all had our saunas and the tree had been trimmed, they enjoyed *lipeäkala* (lutefisk [codfish]) smothered in white sauce, laced with black pepper, and served with boiled potatoes. Our mother had soaked the stiff lutefisk in a pail of water for several days to soften it. We children didn't care for this. A special pastry called a *torttu* (tart) was prepared for Christmastime. These were usually saved for company when we children could enjoy them, too. Sweetened, cooked prune pulp was placed in the center of a small, rolled-out square of rich, flaky pastry. The square was cut diagonally at the corners and the pastry folded over the prune paste in a star-like shape, and baked. The great *torttu* artist in my memory was Mary Kivipelto of Ely. Her *torttus* were the lightest, the flakiest, the most delicious to come out of any Finnish kitchen I knew.

FOOD TRADITIONS OF FINLAND

East meets West in Finnish cuisine. Both Russia and Sweden have influenced Finland's dishes, with the Swedish influence being the stronger, but eating habits differ with regions. The Russian influence sets Finland apart from the rest of Scandinavia.

An eastern Finn, closer geographically to Russia, is likely to lunch on a meat or fish-filled pasty and borscht served with sour cream. A western Finn prefers a smorgasbord followed by a hot dish.

Bread baking was affected by Finland's close ties with the East, too. In western Finland, bread was typically baked in large quantities and infrequently. People ate dried bread until it ran out. The loss of Karelia to the Soviet Union in World War II brought refugees who resettled throughout the rest of Finland. These people ate only fresh bread baked once a week. Western Finnish housewives complained that the refugees were wearing out the ovens by so much baking.

Summer is berry-picking time. Arctic cloudberries, strawberries, blueberries, and lingonberries flourish. Finns are avid mushroom hunters in spring and fall. Gardens yield fresh vegetables and potatoes. Fresh fish, caught in the Baltic, are sold straight from the docks. Fish is eaten raw, pickled, or smoked. Wild game is hunted in forest-covered Finland.

In winter, along with home-canned fruits, vegetables, and whole-grain breads, Finns eat roe (fish eggs) and blinis, a crêpe served with diced onions, melted butter, pepper, and sour cream. It is typical Russian fare.

Tea time on weekday evenings, around 8:30 p.m., is customary in many Finnish homes. Tea is served with open-faced sandwiches, cookies, rolls, pasties, rusks, and marmalade. Other drinks include coffee, cocoa, and hot berry juice with raisins. Entertaining guests at home with a dinner party is just the beginning of a long evening with cocktails and conversation. The hostess frequently serves a late night snack of herring, sausage, cheese, onion soup, or borscht, accompanied by vodka and beer.

The Christmas season is a gastronomic delight. Eating is as festive as decorating the home and exchanging gifts. Christmas Eve dinner begins with appetizers of slightly salted salmon, roe, smoked whitefish, and herring served with several sauces. Fish is followed by cold cuts and salads. Sometimes a pasty and bouillon are served, followed by the main dish. Turkey is becoming a popular main dish, too, with the traditional rutabaga casserole prepared a day in advance. A carrot casserole, peas, prunes, and liver are served, too. Desserts include rice pudding, prune pudding, and a fruit salad or fruit soup. Leftovers are used through the next few days. Christmas baking is important in every household. Traditional ginger cookies baked far ahead of time because they get better with age, raisin cakes, fruit tarts, and *pulla* are typical. The one food that does appear in every home is the braided coffee bread *pulla*.

The aroma of the baked goods adds to the festivities of decorating the Christmas tree, lighting candles and filling vases with fresh flowers. When Finns go visiting, they take a fresh flower to their hosts. The Finns' Christmas Eve celebration includes taking a sauna.

A light meal is served as New Year's Eve supper, to leave room for the midnight snack. The menu is often Finnish elk soup, apple pie, and vanilla custard with coffee. The midnight snack includes roast beef, baked potatoes, relishes, and pickles.

On February 5, Finns honor their national poet, Runeberg. Runeberg tarts, pastries made with breadcrumbs and raspberry jam, were favorites of the poet's wife, Fredrika.

Laskiainen is a traditional time for an outdoor party. Lanterns are hung in trees while people go sledding. After playing, Finns head indoors to warm up and eat a traditional pre-Lenten meal of pea soup; *pannukakku*, or pancake; pigs feet; Shrove Tuesday buns; and cocoa.

During Easter, children dye eggs and homes are decorated with pussy willows and spring greens. The Eastern Orthodox Church influences the Easter dishes. Roast lamb and potatoes are the main course. *Mämmi*, a sweet baked malt dish, and Easter *pasha* are desserts.

Though the last sleet may still be falling on May 1, May Day, a national holiday for students and workers, is considered the first day of spring. Traditional snacks are *tippaleipä* (a fritter) and *sima* (mead) to drink. Herring and icy schnapps are served together.

The Midsummer Eve meal in June is often served outdoors. Summer salads, new potatoes, fresh rhubarb pudding, and whitefish or smoked ham are served on flower-decked tables strewn with birch branches.

Photograph courtesy of Up North Films
Northern Michigan University, Marquette, Michigan

Wooden spoons carved by John Toivonen of Toimi, Minnesota

Two "cities of lakes" are sister cities: Minneapolis, Minnesota, and Kuopio, one of Finland's most modern cities, which celebrated its 200th anniversary in 1982. The cities have an art exchange, and medical schools of the University of Minnesota and the University of Kuopio also have an exchange. Women from America and Finland got together in Kuopio in June 1985, for a "Reunion of Sisters," and reconvened in Minnesota in 1986. Seinäjoki in Finland is a sister city of both Virginia and Duluth, Minnesota.

Elaine Ahlgren of Duluth, Minnesota, wears a costume from Ilmajoki, western Finland, and carries a basket of Finnish bread.

ELAINE'S HERITAGE

Elaine's father, Levi Komula, was born in Chassell, Michigan, and died in 1983 at age 90. Her mother, Saima Esther Honkala, was born in Atlantic Mine, Michigan, and died in 1976 at the age of 72.

"My father spoke of eating oatmeal three times a day as a child as food was not always in abundance. Summers were better times with garden produce. My mother ate chicken for two weeks when her father took chickens to market and the storekeeper didn't need them. She couldn't eat chicken as an adult, but she prepared it for the family.

"My family faced famine and starvation in Finland. I feel my family history is one of much hardship, but that Finnish *sisu* keeps the people strong in their faith and cheerful and thankful to be Americans." Elaine's favorite tales are about her great-grandmother.

"Ruisleipä, rye bread, is the most loved bread of Finland," Beatrice Ojakangas writes. "It is sometimes called 'reikäleipä,' or bread with a hole." This bread and other treats displayed on a Finnish woven cloth were baked by Beatrice Ojakangas and photographed in her kitchen.

A cardamom coffee braid
called pulla *is shown with
pig-shaped cookies in
the center.*

Karpalo

Joulutortut,
*Christmas prune-
filled tarts, are
shown against a
wall hanging from
Finland owned by
Elaine Ahlgren.*
Karpalo,
*embroidered at
the top, means
"cranberry."*

THE TURKU *TORI*

Photographs
by Gerry Kangas

92–

TRADITIONAL FINNISH FOODS
Favored by the Finns
by Beatrice Ojakangas

Beatrice Ojakangas, food and recipe editor for Fantastically Finnish, *was cooking before she could read. The oldest of ten children, she handled many of the cooking responsibilities in their farm home kitchen. Her interest in cooking continued through years of 4-H, completion of a B.S. degree in home economics, and as the author of many acclaimed cookbooks.*

Finns have always appreciated basic, straightforward, natural flavors, textures, and appearances in their food. Food is a gift to be tampered with as little as possible so the God-given flavors remain true, and the nutritional qualities stay high. This does not mean that Finnish food is dull! Finnish food nourishes the soul as well as the body. Just ask a Finn about his favorite food remembered from childhood and you may listen to a tale of simmered soups, baking breads, hearty rice puddings, fresh fish, and stewed meats.

Whole grains, exemplified in their breads and porridges, fresh vegetables, potatoes, wild berries, mushrooms, game, and fish all figure highly in the Finnish diet. Soups are hearty though sometimes delicate. My favorite is the *kesäkeitto,* made ideally in the fleeting moment when the garden produces tender young vegetables that can be simmered in cream and savored for all their natural flavors.

The recipes in this collection came to mind as favorites of my childhood, my parents' childhood, our contributors, and from my experiences traveling in Finland. For American-born Finns, there may be many degrees of nostalgia, too! As a Finnish hostess would say as she invites her guests to the table, *"Olkaa hyvä!"* "Happy cooking!"

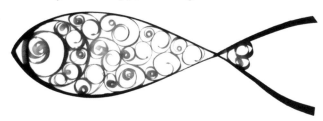

Lastucraft fish made from pine shavings. The Ladies of Kaleva of Virginia, Minnesota, made the traditional and original designs shown in this book. The Finnish term "lastutöitä" *translates as* "lastuwork."

Appetizers and Beverages

When we think of appetizers and beverages, we think of parties! Parties that are centered on appetizers and beverages are more "big city" than part of the rural scene. Perhaps the favorite of first course foods in Finland is fish in one form or another. Fresh caviar spread on bread with sour cream and chopped onion, and a variety of pickled and salted herrings and salmon are delicious. Excellent cheeses, smoked reindeer, breads, fresh vegetables, pâtés, and some meat dishes are part of the appetizer scene in Finland. Meatballs (in the Main Dish section), *Karjalanpiirakat* (in the Pastry section), salmon pies, and veal loaf are all items that may be on an appetizer buffet table. Coupled with the excellent breads in that group, there are lots of ideas for parties!

A favorite Finnish beverage is milk. Buttermilk and *viili,* a clabbered milk, are included. Excellent non-alcoholic beer is served throughout the country, and a very light home-brew, *kalja,* is especially popular in the summertime. *Sima,* a sparkly beverage, is classic for May Day celebrations, and is served with *tippaleipä,* a fried cruller.

Sima

Sima (mead) is the May Day drink of Finland. It is served with tippaleipä, *a crispy fried cruller.*

4 quarts water
1 cup brown sugar
1-1/8 cups granulated sugar, divided
2 lemons
1/8 teaspoon active dry yeast
1 tablespoon raisins

Heat the water to boiling and stir in the brown sugar and 1 cup of the granulated sugar. With peeler, remove zest from the lemons and add to the mixture. Peel away white part of lemon rind and slice the flesh of the lemon into thin slices; add to the mixture. Cool mixture to 100°F and transfer to a non-metallic container (a large plastic bucket is fine). Add yeast and stir. Let stand overnight or at least 8 to 10 hours in a warm place. There should be tiny bubbles around the edge of the liquid after that length of time.

Sterilize 8 pint bottles, 4 quart bottles, or a 1-gallon jug and place 1 to 2 teaspoons sugar per quart of liquid into each container along with 3 to 4 raisins. Strain the liquid and pour it into the containers. Cork tightly. Let stand at room temperature until raisins have risen to the top of the bottle to indicate that the *sima* has fermented enough and is ready to drink. In the winter, this may take 2 days or more; in warm

94–

weather, only 8 hours. Chill and store in the refrigerator or in a cool place. Makes 1 gallon.

Mountain Ash Berry Liqueur
Pihjalanmarjaviini

Jukka Marmo, Finland
In northern climates, the mountain ash trees produce juicy red berries in the fall. It is common for Europeans to use the juice from these berries to make jellies and a bitter type of liqueur. Jukka, a Finnish geologist and gourmet cook, says that the berries must be frosted before using, or put in the freezer overnight to develop the right flavor.

1 cup mountain ash berries, which have been frozen
1 cup sugar
1 cup water
1 quart clear spirits (everclear or vodka)

Wash the berries and pick off stems. Put into a non-aluminum saucepan and add the sugar and water (there should be just enough to cover the berries). Bring **just** to a boil and remove from heat. Cool. Put the cooled berries into a jar and add the spirits. Cover and age for 6 or more months, shaking the jar periodically. Pour through a sieve. This makes an orange-colored liqueur.

Home Brew
Kalja

Kalja, *a non-alcoholic beer, is popular in Finland. It is served with meals and after a sauna. Rye malt may be purchased from whole foods cooperatives or natural food stores. Use a large, clean plastic pail to prepare* kalja.

1 cup rye malt
1 cup sugar
5 quarts boiling water
1 teaspoon dry yeast

Mix the malt and sugar in the bottom of a pail; pour in the boiling water. When water has cooled to about 110°F, add the yeast. Cover with plastic wrap and allow to ferment at room temperature overnight. The next day, strain and bottle. Keep chilled until ready to serve.

Finnish Fireball

Aimo Tervakoski
Silver Spring, Maryland

Ice cubes
Vodka
Cranberry juice

Put 2 or 3 ice cubes into a 6-ounce glass. Add 2 ounces of vodka. Fill balance of glass with cranberry juice and stir. Serves 1.

Tradition says homemade beverages are best when made and shared with the "devoted."

Reindeer Tears
Poron kyyneleet

Aimo Tervakoski
Silver Spring, Maryland
Born in Haapajärvi, Finland, Aimo moved to the United States in 1969, and married a northern Minnesota Finnish American. He operates the import shop Memories of Finland and is part owner of Finlandia Importers, a major importer of Finnish gifts and sauna items.

Whole cranberries
Vodka

Place 2 or 3 whole cranberries into a 2-ounce cordial or liqueur glass. Fill with vodka, say *"kippis"* ("cheers") and drink up!

Banana-Grape Punch
Mehubooli

This innocent punch is popular at family celebrations.

2 quarts bottled grape or
    currant juice, white or red
2 quarts sparkling water or
    club soda
1 quart lemon-flavored soda
2 quarts ice cubes
1 banana, thinly sliced
1 lemon, thinly sliced

Chill all ingredients separately except the banana and lemon. At serving time, pour grape juice, sparkling water, and lemon soda over the ice cubes in a chilled punch bowl. Float banana and lemon slices on top. Makes 32 servings of 5 or 6 ounces each.

Finlandia Punch
Liisanbooli

Liisa Vitali, jewelry designer and fabulous cook in Finland, served this punch in a huge glass battery jar; the effect was dramatic! The punch is "lethal!"

4 parts sweet vermouth
1 part Finlandia vodka
3 parts water
Ice
Lemon strips

Combine the vermouth, vodka, and water and chill. About 1/2 hour before the party pour over ice into a large glass punch bowl. The effect is dramatic if the bowl is very big and deep, but the punch fills only about 1/4 of it. Garnish with lemon strips.

────────────

Finlandia Ski Race

The Finlandia Ski Race, held in February in Finland, has drawn as many as 14,000 cross-country skiers. There are seven categories of competition and a challenging 47-mile course. For information, write the Finnish Tourist Board in New York City.

Salted Salmon
Graavilohi

Gravlox *is the commonly known name for this classic dish. Good cooks in Finland prepare their own salt- and sugar-preserved salmon using fresh fish. Fresh whitefish, salmon, lake trout, or pike can be prepared using this method. The fish is coated with a mixture of salt, sugar, and dill. The fish "cooks" without heat, becomes firm, and changes to a rich reddish-gold color. A weight placed on the salmon to compress the flesh makes it cut easily into thin slices. After mari-nating, the fish is cut on a wide diag-onal into slices, then curled into coils and served with sour cream on thinly sliced dark rye bread.*

10 tablespoons sugar
4 tablespoons salt
2 pounds fresh fish fillets,
skinned (salmon, whitefish,
lake trout, or pike)
4 tablespoons dill weed

Combine the sugar and salt. Rub the fish with the sugar and salt mix-ture. Sprinkle with dill weed. Place into a shallow 13 x 9-inch dish. Top with plastic wrap or waxed paper and weight down (use a board topped with canned foods, milk cartons, etc.). Refrigerate 2 days. Remove weight. Drain off salt and sugar mixture. Slice fish into thin diagonal slices. Serve garnished with fresh dill. Excellent served on thinly sliced dark rye bread with sour cream.

Fresh Caviar Appetizer
Mätiä alkupalana

The roe from any fresh fish can be eaten as an appetizer. This is a delicious treat overlooked by many sports fishermen!

Fresh fish roe
Salt and pepper
Sliced dark rye bread or
pumpernickel
Butter
Sour cream
Chopped green onion
Allspice (optional)

Carefully remove the membranes encasing the roe of any fish. Season the roe with salt and pepper. Turn into a bowl. Spread slices of a dark rye bread or pumpernickel with butter, then with sour cream. Top with a generous coating of the fresh fish roe. Top with chopped green onion and allspice if desired. Eat with a knife and fork or simply "out of hand."

Along with summer, family, friends, a cottage and a sauna by the lake, and a favorite drink, another pastime of the Finns is dancing, with the tango being the dance of choice.

Rabbit-Liver Pâté
Jänispasteija

Soile Anderson
North Oaks, Minnesota
Soile comes from Kerimäki, Finland,
a city in eastern Finland. She owns
the Taste of Scandinavian bakeries in
the Twin Cities.

1 pound veal or chicken liver
1/2 pound ground pork
1 pound rabbit meat, deboned
    and ground
2 onions, chopped
2 cloves garlic
2 tablespoons salt
White pepper to taste
Allspice to taste
2 cups heavy cream
Fresh parsley, finely chopped
Bacon slices

Grind meats, except bacon, together.
Sauté onions and garlic; cool and
mix with meat. Add spices and mix
all ingredients, adding heavy cream.
Cover baking pan with strips of
bacon and fill with pâté mixture.
Place a few strips of bacon on top of
pâté. Put baking pan inside pan of
water in the oven and bake at 250°F
for 2 hours. Let cool slightly before

Gerry Kangas photographed this plate
of neula muikku, small smelt-like fish
served in the Midsummer buffet at the
Kalevala Hotel in Kuhmo.

unmolding from pan. Serve this
pâté hot or cold. Excellent served
with lingonberries.

Finnish Salted Herring
Suolasilli

This is a dish that is always there on
the Finnish voileipäpöytä. *It is usually*
presented with different toppings; you
may take your choice.

1 large salt herring
Chopped green onion
Chopped hard-cooked eggs
Chopped parsley
Chopped pickled beets
Capers
Sour cream

Cut the fish into fillets and soak
overnight in cold water to cover.
Remove skin and bones. Rinse and
drain. Cut into 1/4-inch slices crosswise. Arrange on serving platter.
Offer with small bowls full of
chopped green onion, hard-cooked
eggs, parsley, pickled beets, capers,
and sour cream. One herring serves
about 4 people for appetizers.

Soups

Soups and stews are among the favorites of Finnish meals. Basically, the varieties are much alike—based usually on potatoes, meat, or fish. As is typical of most cuisines of the world, every cook has his or her own version of classic soups and stews. In this collection, we have a sampling of the favorite varieties.

Pea Soup
Hernekeitto

"This is perfect for freezing," says Edna E. Johnson, Aurora, Minnesota. *Soup can be made in advance and reheated. Most people feel soup tastes even better the next day when reheated. Serve with hardtack, rye crisp, or homemade bread. Fresh or canned fruit is an ideal way to finish the meal.*

**2 cups whole dried yellow
      peas, or 1 cup whole dried
      yellow peas and 1 cup split
      yellow peas
2 quarts water
6 whole allspice
2 cups cubed ham or 1 ham bone
      with meat on it
1 cup diced carrots
1/4 cup diced onion
2 cups diced potatoes
1 teaspoon salt
Dash pepper**

Rinse whole peas and cover with water. Soak overnight (do not soak split peas). Next day, drain peas. Simmer peas, allspice, and ham bone in 2 quarts of water for 1 hour or until pea skins pop. Remove bone, scraping meat into soup. Add carrots, onion, potatoes, salt, and pepper and simmer over low heat for 1 hour. If using cubed ham, add meat during second hour. Makes 3 quarts soup, 10 to 12 servings.

Old Karelian Barley and Mushroom Soup
Ohra-tattikeitto

**1/3 cup uncooked pearl
      barley
5 cups beef broth or water
1 teaspoon salt or to taste
1/2 pound mushrooms, sliced
1-1/2 cups light cream (half
      milk, half cream)
1 tablespoon butter**

Simmer barley in broth for 1 hour until tender. Add salt, mushrooms, and cream. Simmer 15 minutes longer. Top with butter. Serve hot. Makes 8 servings.

Finnish Beer Cheese Soup

Kaljakeitto

2 cups milk
2 tablespoons all-purpose
    flour
1 tablespoon sugar
Salt to taste
1/2 cup dark Finnish-style beer
1/2 cup beef broth
1 tablespoon dark corn syrup
1/4 teaspoon ground ginger
2 cups diced Emmenthaler
    (Finnish-style) Swiss cheese

In a saucepan, combine milk, flour, and sugar. Heat to a boil, stirring. Cook, stirring until thickened. Remove from heat. In another saucepan, combine beer, broth, corn syrup, and ginger. Heat to boiling, stirring constantly. Stir into thickened milk mixture. Return to heat. Heat to boiling. Place cheese in bottom of soup bowls or tureen. Ladle soup into bowls and serve immediately. Makes 6 servings.

Finnish Hospitality
Inviting guests for a sauna is as common as inviting them for a meal.

Summer Soup

Kesäkeitto

Esther Luoma, Duluth, Minnesota

1 quart water
2 teaspoons salt
1 cup tiny new carrots,
    scrubbed
1 cup tiny new potatoes,
    scrubbed until peel
    comes off
1 cup new green beans, sliced
    diagonally
1 cup fresh green peas
1/2 cup chopped fresh
    spinach
2 tablespoons all-purpose
    flour
1 quart milk
3 tablespoons butter
1/4 cup chopped parsley

Bring water and salt to a boil in a soup pot. Add carrots and potatoes and simmer until about half-cooked, 10 minutes. Add the green beans, peas, and spinach. Cook another 10 minutes until all vegetables are just tender; do not overcook. Mix flour with a little of the milk to make a smooth paste. Stir into hot soup. Add remaining milk and simmer soup for 10 minutes. Remove from heat and stir in butter and parsley. Makes 6 servings.

Milk Potatoes
Maitoperunat

Karen and Roger Mattson
Duluth, Minnesota
This is what Finns tend to choose to eat when they "don't know what they want to eat." Maitoperunat *is a satisfying, nourishing, inexpensive soup made with small new potatoes and ranks among the "heavenly foods." Karen and Roger Mattson say that the new potato version is one they use in July, August, and September, when the new potatoes are available.*

3 pounds small new potatoes (or six older potatoes, medium-sized, peeled and diced)
4 small new onions (or 1 large older onion, peeled and diced)
Water to cover
1 cup cream or whole milk
Salt and pepper to taste
Good-sized lump of butter

Scrub the small new potatoes and place into a soup pot with the onions. Cover with water and simmer just until the potatoes can be pierced with a toothpick. Add cream, salt, and pepper and dot with butter. Serve immediately. Makes 6 servings.

Meat Stew
Lihamojakka

This is the corollary of the fish stew known also by the name of mojakka, that nonexistent word in the true Finnish language! Some people like to add tomatoes at the very end. Others prefer not to have the mojakka made with anything but meat and potatoes!

1-1/2 pounds beef for stewing
4 cups water
1 onion, sliced or chopped
6 whole allspice or whole black pepper
6 carrots (optional), pared and diced
6 potatoes, pared and diced
Salt to taste

In a heavy soup pot or Dutch oven, brown the meat in just enough butter or oil to keep from sticking. (Some people prefer not to brown the meat at all but simply place it in the pot with the water and onion.) Add the water, onion, and allspice or pepper and simmer slowly until meat is very tender and begins to fall apart, about 1-1/2 to 2 hours. Add carrots and potatoes. Simmer until vegetables are tender. Taste and add salt. Makes 4 to 6 servings.

Finnish Dumplings
Klimpit

Ethel Saari Wuori
Elk River, Minnesota

1 egg, slightly beaten
1 tablespoon melted
shortening or oil
1/2 cup milk
3/4 cup all-purpose flour
1/2 teaspoon salt
1/2 cup raisins, softened in
hot water

Beat egg. Add shortening and milk; stir in the flour and salt and beat vigorously until smooth. Stir in the raisins. Drop by tablespoonsful into hot boiling soup. (Note: Dip spoon into the boiling soup before dipping into the batter; thus dumplings will drop off easily.) Simmer until dumplings rise to the top.

Breads of Finland

Breads are the mainstay of the Finnish diet. Rye is the most popular grain, and a soured rye bread is what homesick Finns long for when they are on extended visits away from Finland. If there's no bread in the house, a Finn would complain, "There's nothing to eat!" A meal without bread is almost unthinkable!

Finnish-American cooks also are great bread bakers. Finnish breads differ from other Scandinavian and European rye breads in that they generally are less sweet and are made with a coarser rye flour. Flat breads called *rieska,* made with barley, rye, oats, and other whole grains, are delicious! The thickness of the flat bread varies depending on which part of Finland the original recipe came from. They are usually about the size and shape of a pizza and are cut into wedges, served hot with butter. Breads that are baked for special occasions, such as the holidays or for serving on the coffee table, include sugar. Sweetened and spiced rye bread is typical of Christmas bread, and sweetened cardamom-flavored coffee bread is served with coffee.

Many old-timers in America have known the cardamom-flavored coffee bread as *nisu* while others call it *pulla* or *vehnä* or biscuit. The recipe is the same. The name varies. *Nisu* is the old-fashioned Finnish word for wheat. Today wheat is called *vehnä;* hence those two names for the bread. *Pulla* is the common name for the same bread and is actually related to the name that Sweden uses for the same bread, *bullar.*

Finnish Rye Bread
Hiivaleipä

Ebba M. Hill, Aurora, Minnesota, learned to bake from her mother who baked for the family bakery. When the family moved to the country, as was traditional, the first building was the sauna. Into the sauna, her father built a large brick oven. There her mother baked breads for the week as the sauna heated for the big family. She remembers the delicious smell of the fresh breads as her mother pulled them from the big oven with the long-handled wooden spatula. She always baked a variety of breads, sweet rolls, and braids.

1 package active dry yeast
1/2 cup warm water (110°F)
1-1/2 cups hot water
2 tablespoons honey
2 teaspoons salt
1/4 cup butter or margarine
3 cups medium rye flour
2 cups all-purpose flour
Melted butter

In a small bowl, dissolve the yeast in the 1/2 cup warm water. In a large bowl, combine the hot water, honey, salt, and butter. Cool to lukewarm. Add yeast mixture and rye flour. Beat with wooden spoon until smooth. Work in the white flour, adding more if necessary to make a soft dough. Knead until smooth and elastic, about 10 minutes. Put into a warmed, greased bowl, turning to grease dough all around. Place in a warm place to rise until doubled, about 1 hour. Punch down and let rest 10 minutes. Form into 2 loaves and place into well-greased 9 x 5-inch loaf pans. Cover and let rise until doubled, about 45 minutes. Bake at 400°F about 30 minutes or until brown on top and loaf sounds "hollow" when tapped on bottom. Brush tops with melted butter.

Shrove Tuesday Buns
Laskiaispullat

Natalie Saari Gallagher, St. Paul
As a final fling before Lent, everyday pulla *takes on a festive look and taste. Ready-to-use almond paste (marzipan) brings an old recipe up to date and makes it easy to prepare.*

6 to 8 *pulla* buns (make *pulla* [p. 106] and shape into buns)
1 roll (3-1/2 ounce) almond paste
1/4 cup soft butter or margarine
1/2 cup cream, whipped

Cut the top off each *pulla* bun about 1/3 of the way down from the top. Scoop out a bit of the inside of each bun. For filling, thoroughly beat together the almond paste and butter. Fill the buns with this mixture. Whip the cream until thick and put a dollop of whipped cream on top of the filling; cover with the *pulla* cap or lid.

Emergency Bread
Hätäleipä

Hätä *means "emergency" in Finnish, and* leipä *translates to "bread." "I remember growing up and my mother talking about* hätäleipä. *It's the kind that you just stir up, turn out onto a prepared baking sheet, and let rise for 30 minutes or so. Much quicker than running to the store for a loaf of bread."*   —Beatrice Ojakangas

**1 package active dry yeast
1 cup warm water (105°–115°F)
2 tablespoons molasses
1 tablespoon oil, melted lard,
    bacon drippings, or butter
1 teaspoon salt
1/2 cup stone ground rye
    flour, pumpernickel rye, or
    light rye flour
1-1/2 cups bread flour or
    all-purpose flour
Butter to brush top of loaf**

In mixing bowl, dissolve yeast in the water; add molasses; let stand 3 to 5 minutes until yeast foams. Stir in oil, salt, and rye flour. Stir in bread flour, then beat 50 times. Cover a baking sheet with parchment paper or grease generously. Turn dough out onto the sheet, spreading it into a circle about 8 inches in diameter. Let rise 30 minutes. Bake in a 400°F oven for 20 minutes or until center of loaf springs back when touched. Serve hot, cut into wedges, and split horizontally. Makes 1 loaf.

104–

Potato and Barley Flat Bread
Peruna-ohrarieska

There is a great variety of Finnish flat breads. They vary in thickness depending on which part of the country the original recipe comes from. Rieska *is always best served hot out of the oven at which time it is quite flexible and tender. As it cools and ages,* rieska *becomes chewy.*

**1 cup buttermilk
1 cup mashed potatoes
1/2 cup melted butter
1 teaspoon salt
1 teaspoon baking soda
1 cup barley flour
2 cups uncooked rolled oats
2 cups all-purpose flour
Butter**

Combine all ingredients in mixing bowl in the order listed. Stir to make a smooth dough. Turn out onto barley-floured board and divide into four parts. Roll each part out to make a circle 10 to 12 inches in diameter. Place on greased baking sheet and pierce all over with a fork. Bake at 450°F for 10 minutes. Brush with melted butter. Serve hot. Makes 4 loaves.

Graham Rusks
Grahamkorput

These are twice-baked buns, baked a second time to completely dry out the split breads so that they keep well. Ideal for summertime picnics, cabin fare, and lunches.

3 packages active dry yeast
1/4 cup warm water
(105°–115°F)
2 cups buttermilk
1/2 cup melted butter or
melted lard
2 teaspoons salt
2 teaspoons caraway seed
3 cups graham flour or
whole-wheat flour
3 to 3-1/2 cups bread flour or
all-purpose flour

In large bowl, dissolve yeast in the warm water. Heat buttermilk to about 110°F. Mix buttermilk, butter, salt, caraway seed, and graham flour into yeast mixture. Beat until smooth; cover. Let rise in a warm place until mixture develops a sponge-like texture, about 1 hour. Stir in enough all-purpose flour to make dough easy to handle. Turn onto lightly floured board. Knead until smooth and elastic, about 10 minutes; cover. Let rest 15 minutes. Divide dough in half; divide each half into quarters. Shape each piece into three parts to make 24 equal pieces. Shape into smooth round balls. Place on lightly greased baking sheets. Flatten slightly. Cover and let rise until doubled, about 1 hour. Bake in a 375°F oven for 20 to 25 minutes. Cool on wire racks. Split horizontally in halves using two forks (don't cut them). Place on baking sheets and toast in a 300°F oven until dry and crisp, about 5 minutes. Makes 24 buns, 48 rusks.

Finnish Flat Barley Bread
Rieska

Finnish Cultural Center
Farmington Hills, Michigan

3 cups all-purpose flour
1-3/4 cups barley or graham
flour
1 tablespoon sugar
1 tablespoon baking powder
2 teaspoons salt
1/2 cup shortening
2 cups buttermilk
1 teaspoon baking soda

Combine dry ingredients except for the soda. Cut shortening into dry ingredients with pastry blender until mixture resembles coarse crumbs. Blend buttermilk and soda and stir into the dry ingredients until a soft dough forms. Pat onto a greased 14 x 17-inch cookie sheet to about 1/2-inch thickness. Bake at 425°F for 20 minutes or until slightly brown. Makes 1 flat loaf.

Cardamom Coffee Bread
Pulla

Marilyn R. Hoisve
Plymouth, Minnesota
Serve this bread sliced, with "egg-cleared" coffee. It is a must for all special occasions.

7 whole cardamom pods
2 cups milk
1 package active dry yeast
2 eggs
3/4 cup sugar
1/2 cup butter or margarine, softened
2 teaspoons salt
6-1/2 to 7 cups all-purpose flour, divided

For glaze:
1 egg, beaten
1/2 cup sliced almonds
Coarse sugar

Crack open cardamom pods and heat in a small pan for several minutes. Grind or pound seeds and set aside. Heat milk to lukewarm. Add yeast and stir until dissolved. In a large mixing bowl, beat eggs and sugar until foamy. Add milk, cardamom, and 2 cups flour. Beat at medium speed for 2 minutes until smooth and elastic. Stir in softened butter, salt, and enough flour to make dough stiff enough to knead. Knead on floured surface until smooth and satiny, about 5 to 10 minutes. Place in a greased bowl, turning to grease top. Cover; let rise in warm place until light and doubled in size. On floured surface divide dough into three parts. Divide each third into three parts. Form each part into a strip 16 inches long. Braid three together, sealing ends. Repeat for remaining 2 loaves. Place on greased cookie sheets. Cover loosely and let rise about 30 minutes until less than doubled in size. Brush loaves with egg; sprinkle with almonds and sugar. Bake at 375°F for 20 to 25 minutes. Makes 3 loaves.

Lingonberries

Throughout the ages, the Finnish diet has been "functional," relying on oats, barley, and other crops dried for the winter. Berries picked in the summer were preserved. In early spring, cranberries were found under the snow. If crops failed, pine bark was added to the bread or fresh new spruce shoots were eaten. Milk was preserved by fermentation. These methods of preserving the nutritional function of foods are being scientifically proven today. Finland is noted as a world leader in the development of functional or health-enhancing foods. Scientists have even conducted research on the health-enhancing effects of the old pine bark bread.

106–

Finnish Christmas Rye Bread

Joululimppu

Mrs. Aune Flaada
Makinen, Minnesota

2 cups rye flour
1 quart mashed potatoes
2 cups potato water
1 large cake fresh yeast or
   1 ounce dry yeast
   dissolved in 1/4 cup
   warm water
1-1/2 cups dark molasses
5 cups warm water
1/2 cup oil
1/2 cup sugar
3 tablespoons salt
1 tablespoon anise seed
1 cup golden raisins
2 cups rye flour
18 to 20 cups all-purpose flour

In a large bowl, combine 2 cups rye flour, mashed potatoes, potato water, and yeast. Stir and cover. Let stand at room temperature for 2 days.

Stir in the molasses, warm water, oil, sugar, salt, anise, raisins, and rye flour. Add all-purpose flour to make a stiff dough. Turn out onto floured surface and knead until dough loses its stickiness. Place into greased bowl; let rise in a warm place until doubled. Shape into loaf or round pans. Let rise until doubled. Bake at 375°F for about 40 to 50 minutes or until loaf sounds hollow when tapped. Makes 9 to 10 loaves.

Sour Rye Bread

Hapanleipä

2 packages active dry yeast,
   divided
2 cups warm water (105°–115°),
   divided
3 cups rye flour
1 teaspoon salt
3 to 3-1/2 cups bread flour or
   unbleached all-purpose flour
Soft butter

In a large bowl, dissolve 1 package of the yeast in 1-3/4 cups of the warm water. Stir in the rye flour; cover. Let stand in a warm place until mixture develops a distinctive sour aroma, 24 to 36 hours.

Dissolve the second package of yeast in the remaining 1/4 cup warm water and add to the rye mixture. Add salt and stir in enough bread flour to make a stiff dough. Let rest 10 minutes. Place in greased bowl; turn greased side up and cover. Let rise in a warm place until doubled, about 2 hours. Punch down. Divide in half. Shape each half into a ball. Place on greased baking sheets. Flatten into 12-inch circles. Cut or pull a 2-inch hole in the center of each circle. Cover. Let rise in warm place until doubled, about 1 hour. Heat oven to 375°F. Pierce loaves all over with a fork. Bake until golden brown, 25 to 30 minutes. Brush with butter; cover with towel to soften crust. Cool; cut into wedges, then split horizontally. Makes 2 loaves.

Farmer Rye Bread
Ruisleipä

This bread is popular with Finnish-American bakers. In Finland, the same dough is allowed to stand until the dough sours, producing a sour rye bread. It is important to use the coarser rye meal or pumpernickel rye, sometimes called "dark rye" or "stone ground rye."

1 package active dry yeast
1/4 cup warm water (105°–115°F)
1 cup warm potato water
**   or milk (105°–115°F)**
1 tablespoon brown sugar
1-1/2 cups rye meal, pumper-
**   nickel rye, or dark rye flour**
1 tablespoon melted butter
1-1/2 teaspoons salt
2 cups unbleached all-purpose
**   flour**
Butter

The birch tree and granite are Finland national nature symbols.

In a large mixing bowl, dissolve the yeast in the 1/4 cup warm water. Add the potato water or milk and brown sugar. Mix in the rye meal, melted butter, and salt and beat well. Stir in enough additional flour to make a stiff dough. Let dough rest for 15 minutes. Turn out onto lightly rye-flour-covered board and knead for 10 minutes or until dough is very smooth. Rye bread dough may always retain a "tackiness," but resist the temptation to add too much flour, which will make a very heavy bread. Wash bowl, grease it, and add dough to bowl. Turn over to grease top. Cover and let rise in a warm place until doubled; it may take up to 2 hours. Punch down and shape into one round loaf. Butter an 8- or 9-inch round cake pan. Place dough into the pan with smooth side up. Let rise again until doubled, about 45 minutes to 1 hour. Bake at 375°F for 45 to 50 minutes or until a skewer inserted through the center comes out clean and bread is golden. Brush with butter while hot. Makes 1 loaf.

Finnish Flat Bread

Rieska

Karen Kiviluoma
Aurora, Minnesota
For several years, Karen baked 40 to 50 loaves of this bread for the traditional Laskiainen *festival. She also participated in the American Folklife Festival at the Smithsonian in Washington, D.C. Her recipes were included in the* Festival of American Folklife 1980 Cookbook. *This is her preferred recipe for flat bread.*

4 cups lukewarm water
1/4 cup powdered milk
1 egg, lightly beaten
1/4 cup brown sugar
2 packages active dry yeast
9 to 11 cups all-purpose flour, divided
1/2 cup oatmeal, uncooked
1/2 cup cracked wheat flour
1/2 cup whole-wheat flour
1 tablespoon salt
1/4 cup softened butter or margarine

In a large bowl, add water and powdered milk. Stir to dissolve. Add lightly beaten egg. Stir in brown sugar. Mix the dry yeast with a small amount of white flour and add to the liquid mixture. Add oatmeal, cracked wheat, and whole-wheat flours and a little white flour to make a sponge. Let set for about an hour.

Add salt and beat in all-purpose flour a little at a time, beating after each addition. When stiff dough forms, knead in the softened butter or margarine. Continue kneading until smooth. Cover and let rise for about 45 minutes. Divide dough and place on greased baking sheets. Pat or roll to 1-inch thickness and prick with a fork. Let rise again for about 30 minutes. Bake at 375°F for 30 minutes or until lightly browned. When done, remove from oven and cover with a towel to soften the crust.

Finnish Fennel Seed Rye Bread

Reikäleipä or Limppu

Karen Kiviluoma
Aurora, Minnesota

2 packages active dry yeast
1/4 cup warm water
4 cups buttermilk, heated to lukewarm
1 egg
2 tablespoons honey
1 tablespoon salt
1-1/2 teaspoons fennel seed
5 cups rye flour
8 or more cups all-purpose flour
1/2 cup shortening

In a large bowl, dissolve the yeast in the warm water. Add the buttermilk. Stir in the egg, honey, salt, and fennel seed. Gradually add the rye flour and beat until smooth. Slowly beat in the all-purpose flour to make a stiff dough. Turn dough onto a floured board; knead in the shortening and continue kneading until smooth. Place in a lightly greased bowl, turning to grease the top. Cover lightly and let rise in a warm place until doubled in bulk (1 to 2 hours).

To make *reikäleipä*, divide dough into three parts, shape, and flatten. Place onto a greased baking sheet. Use a cup to make a hole in the center. Prick all over with a fork. Let rise only a short time. Bake at 375°F for 45 to 55 minutes.

To make *limppu*, divide dough into three parts and shape into round loaves. Place into lightly greased 9-inch round cake pans. Prick with a fork. Let rise again until doubled. Bake at 375°F for 45 to 55 minutes or until bread shrinks from sides of the pan. Brush with butter while hot. Cover lightly with clean towels and cool on racks. Makes 3 loaves.

Viipuri Twist
Viipurinrinkilä

This might sound like a new folk dance, but actually it is a pretzel-shaped coffee bread often served during the holiday season in Karelian-Finnish families. Originally this bread was baked on a layer of clean straw.

2 packages active dry yeast
1/4 cup warm water
(105°–115°F)
2 eggs
1 cup sugar
2 cups milk, scalded and cooled
to 105°–115°F
2 teaspoons freshly ground
cardamom
1 teaspoon freshly ground
nutmeg
1-1/2 teaspoons salt
6-1/2 to 7-1/2 cups all-purpose
flour
1/2 cup soft butter
1 egg beaten with 2 tablespoons
milk for glaze
Pearl sugar or crushed loaf sugar
for garnish

Dissolve yeast in the warm water; let stand 2 to 3 minutes until bubbly. Stir in eggs, sugar, milk, cardamom, nutmeg, and salt. Mix until blended. Gradually add flour, beating to keep mixture smooth. Add butter. Stir in remaining flour until dough is very stiff. Cover and let stand 15 minutes. Knead for 10 minutes until smooth and satiny. Place in a lightly oiled bowl. Cover and let rise in a warm place until doubled. Punch down; let rise again for 30 minutes. Divide into three portions. Roll each out to make a long strip about 1 inch in diameter. Shape each strip into a large pretzel. Place on parchment-covered baking sheet. Let rise in a warm place until doubled.

Brush with egg and milk mixture; sprinkle with sugar. Bake at 400°F for 25 to 30 minutes or until light golden brown. Makes 3 loaves.

St. Urho's Day Rye Bread

Pyhän Urhon ruisleipä

This makes one big loaf of bread fragrant with anise, fennel, and orange peel. This bread is firm and close textured—excellent sliced thinly and served with cheese.

1-1/2 cups (12-ounce can) dark beer
1/2 cup milk
2-1/2 cups dark or pumpernickel rye flour
1 cup cracked wheat
2 teaspoons salt
1 teaspoon crushed anise seed
2 teaspoons crushed fennel seed
1 tablespoon grated orange peel
2 packages active dry yeast
1/4 cup warm water (105°–115°F)
1 tablespoon dark corn syrup
2 to 2-1/2 cups bread flour

In saucepan, heat beer and milk to a boil (milk will curdle). Measure rye flour and cracked wheat into large bowl and add boiling mixture. Stir in salt, anise, fennel, and orange peel. Let cool to 105°–115°F. In a small bowl, dissolve yeast in the warm water and add the corn syrup; let stand until foamy, about 5 min-

John Johnson, photograph

St. Urho and grasshopper, both made of fiberglass, Menahga, Minnesota

utes; stir into cooled mixture. Add bread flour gradually to make a stiff dough. Let stand 15 minutes. Turn out onto lightly floured board and knead for 10 minutes until dough is smooth and springy. Wash bowl, grease it, and put dough into bowl. Turn over to grease top, cover, and let rise until doubled, about 1-1/2 to 2 hours. Punch down. Turn out onto lightly oiled surface and shape into a smooth round loaf. Cover baking sheet with parchment paper or lightly grease it. Place loaf on prepared baking pan with smooth side up. Let rise until almost doubled, about 45 minutes to 1 hour. Slash with sharp knife or razor blade in three parallel cuts going each way on the loaf, making 1-inch squares. Preheat oven to 375°F. Bake for 40 to 45 minutes or until loaf sounds hollow when tapped. Makes 1 large loaf.

Finnish Biscuit

Bisketti or *Nisu*

This is the popular bread that is baked weekly in many Finnish-American homes. It is a sweet white bread, flavored with cardamom, braided and baked. Sometimes the dough is shaped into cinnamon rolls or other types of coffee cakes. The popular korppu *or dry toast is made by slicing this bread and rebaking the slices until they are crisp. Some of the old-timers refer to this bread as* nisu, *from the old Swedish-Finnish word for wheat.*

2 packages active dry yeast
3/4 cup warm water
1 can (13-ounce) undiluted
    evaporated milk, heated
    to 110°F
1/2 to 1 cup sugar
2 teaspoons salt
1 teaspoon or more crushed
    cardamom seeds
4 eggs, beaten
8 to 9 cups all-purpose flour
1/2 cup softened butter
Egg mixed with milk for glaze
Pearl sugar, sliced almonds, or
    plain sugar for decoration

Dissolve the yeast in the warm water. Stir in the milk, sugar, salt, cardamom, eggs, and enough flour to make a batter (about 2 cups). Beat until dough is smooth and elastic. Add about 3 cups of the flour and beat well. Dough should be smooth and glossy in appearance. Add remaining flour 1 cup at a time until dough is stiff. Add the butter; beat until dough looks glossy again. Turn out onto floured board, and cover with inverted mixing bowl. Let rest for 15 minutes. Knead until smooth and satiny. Place in a lightly greased bowl, turn dough to grease top, cover lightly, and let rise in a warm place (about 85°F) until doubled. Punch down; let rise again. Turn out onto lightly floured board, divide into three parts and divide each part into three. Shape each piece of dough into a strip 16 inches long by rolling between palms and board. Braid three strips together into a straight loaf and pinch ends together and tuck under. Repeat for second and third loaves. Place on lightly greased baking sheets. Let rise until puffy (1/2 to 1 hour). Glaze loaves with a mixture of beaten egg and milk. Sprinkle with pearl sugar, crushed loaf sugar, and/or sliced almonds. Bake at 400°F for 25 to 30 minutes. Do not overbake or loaves will be dry. Makes 3 loaves.

Lakka *(cloudberries) are tart berries resembling a raspberry, but orange in color. They are used in many ways, from sauces to sorbets. There is also a* Lakka *liqueur.*

Pastries in Finland

Finnish home bakers, especially those of Karelian descent, are pastry bakers. Rye-crusted, rice-filled pies *(Karjalanpiirakka)* are available throughout the country today and are extremely popular. They are eaten as a bread with a light meal of soup or salad. They can be eaten as sandwiches, with a spreading of egg butter, or eaten as snacks. Other varieties of pastries are known, too. A potato filling is less common, but popular with some Finns. Meat and rice-filled turnovers stem also from Karelian background. The north country pasties included in Main Dishes are undoubtedly popular with Finnish Americans because of the native interest in main dish pastries.

Rice-Filled Pastries
Piirakat

Mrs. Ronald (Eila) Isaacson
Virginia, Minnesota

Filling:
1 quart whole milk
1 cup regular rice, cooked
1/2 teaspoon salt
1 cup (1/2 pound) butter

Crust:
3 cups all-purpose flour
1/2 cup shortening (may be part butter)
1 cup water

For the filling, in a large heavy saucepan, add milk slowly to cooked rice. Cook until it begins to thicken, about 1 hour over low heat. It will be slightly liquid. Add the salt and butter. Mix well. Stir and let it cook until very thick.

For the crust, mix the flour and shortening as for pie crust. Add about 1 cup cold water. Knead until it is pliable. Chill overnight. When you are ready to bake, roll out dough and cut into oblong shapes. Put a spoonful or two of rice mixture in the center, pinch the sides to form a shell, and turn the pie into an oval shape. Some of the filling should show from the center. Bake in the oven at 400°F for 45 minutes or until golden brown. After baking, dip or brush the baked *piirakat* in warm glaze of 1-1/2 cups boiling water and 3 tablespoons butter. They should be served warm. Leftovers should be stored in the refrigerator between paper layers in a container.

In Karelia, eastern Finland, some specialties are: Sara, *a mutton and potato dish baked in a wooden trough;* Rantakala, *shore-fish stew;* Rieska *and* Kalakukko, *breads baked with fish and pork. Fine Georgian wines are also specialties of this region.*

–113

Karelian Rye-Crusted Rice-Filled Pastries
Karjalanpiirakat

This Karelian specialty has become so popular in Finland that it can be purchased in bakeries and supermarkets. Traditionally these pastries are served with a topping of hard-cooked egg mixed with butter.

Filling:
1 cup uncooked medium-grain
  rice
2 cups milk
2 tablespoons butter or
  margarine
1 to 2 teaspoons salt
Additional milk if necessary
  to thin out filling

Crust:
1-1/2 cups all-purpose flour
1-1/2 cups rye flour
1 cup water
2 tablespoons butter, melted
1 teaspoon salt

Glaze:
1/2 cup butter, melted
1/2 cup hot milk

Egg Butter:
1 cup softened butter
4 hard-cooked eggs, chopped

To prepare filling, cook rice according to package directions. Stir milk into cooked rice and continue cooking over medium to low heat until mixture is thick and bubbly, about 10 to 15 minutes. Stir in the 2 tablespoons butter. Season with salt. Set aside. As mixture cools it might thicken; add milk if necessary to keep it the consistency of cooked oatmeal.

To prepare crust, combine all-purpose flour and rye flour in mixing bowl. Combine water, butter, and salt and stir into the flour, mixing to make a dough about the consistency of yeast bread dough. Turn out onto board and knead until smooth, about 3 minutes.

Heat oven to 450°F. Shape dough into a roll 2 inches in diameter. Cut into 16 equal pieces. Shape each into a ball. Roll each ball out to make a 6-inch circle. Spread 1/4 cup rice filling in a 3-inch strip across the center of each dough circle almost to the edge. Fold opposite sides over filling. Leave 1 inch of filling exposed in the center. Crimp each edge. Pinch ends to form an oval and seal in the filling. Place *piirakat* on greased baking sheets. Mix the 1/2 cup butter and 1/2 cup hot milk; brush lightly over *piirakat*. Bake, brushing once during baking with the butter-milk mixture. Bake 15 minutes or until light brown. Remove from oven; brush again with milk mixture. To prepare egg butter, mash butter and hard-cooked egg together until blended. Turn into serving bowl. Serve hot or cooled with egg butter spread over the top. Makes 16.

Rye Pastries with Creamy Wheat Filling

Sultsinat

Sultsinat come from the eastern lake district of Finland. The crust for sultsinat is the same as for Karelian piirakat, but sultsinat are cooked much like the Norwegians cook lefse, on a hot griddle. While the sulsinat are hot and pliable, they are spread with a creamy farina mixture and folded so the ends are left open. Sultsinat can be cut into smaller pieces to serve along with cookies or pastries. Sulsinat are delicious served with cinnamon, sugar, and melted butter to dip or sprinkle onto the pastries.

Crust:
1 cup water
2 tablespoons oil
1 teaspoon salt
2 cups rye flour
1 to 1-1/2 cups all-purpose flour

Filling:
2 cups milk
1/3 cup uncooked farina
1 teaspoon salt
3 tablespoons butter or margarine
3 tablespoons sugar
1-1/2 teaspoons ground cinnamon

To serve:
1/2 cup sugar
2 teaspoons ground cinnamon
Cream or melted butter

To make crust, mix water, oil, and 1 teaspoon salt in bowl. Stir in the rye and all-purpose flour. Turn dough onto floured board and knead until smooth, about 5 minutes. Divide into 16 pieces. Roll each out to make an 8-inch circle. Place on preheated ungreased griddle heated to 450°F. Cook 1/2 minute on each side. Stack and keep warm, covered so *sultsinat* stay pliable.

To prepare filling, heat milk to simmering and stir in the farina and 1 teaspoon salt. Cook and stir over medium heat for 1 minute. Remove from heat and cover. Let stand until thick. Stir in butter, 3 tablespoons sugar, and the 1-1/2 teaspoons cinnamon. Spread 2 to 3 tablespoons of the farina filling across the center of each pastry circle from edge to edge. Make 3 folds, one from each side toward the center, and then again in the center so that the *sultsinat* end up with open ends and are long and narrow. Mix the 1/2 cup sugar and 2 teaspoons cinnamon. Serve *sultsinat* with cream and sugar-cinnamon mixture for dipping. Or, cut into diagonal 2-inch-long pieces and arrange on plate or tray to serve. Makes 16.

Finnish Salads

Classic Finnish salads are made from vegetables pretty much limited to beets, carrots, onions, potatoes, cucumbers, mushrooms, and tomatoes. These are the vegetables grown in Finland, and include root vegetables that can be stored throughout the long winter months easily.

Finnish salads in variety are often a colorful assortment on a *voileipäpöytä*, the Finnish counterpart of the Swedish smorgasbord. If you plan to serve a *voileipäpöytä*, any or all of the salads are appropriate at the same time!

Garden lettuce salads were always popular during the summertime, but today with imported foods, the Finnish open market offers lettuce from all over the world any time of year!

Salad dressings are usually simple mixtures of lemon juice, sugar, salt, pepper, and cream or oil.

Herring Salad
Sillisalaatti

This salad is invariably found in the Finnish voileipäpöytä. *It's great served as a first course or as a fish course, as well as for a salad with a light, meatless meal.*

1 jar (12 ounces) herring
    fillets in wine sauce,
    drained
1 cup chopped mild onion
1/2 cup fresh dill or
    4 tablespoons dill weed
1/2 cup heavy cream
Salt
Pepper
Leaf lettuce and lemon wedges

Dice herring; toss with the onion and dill. Whip cream until stiff. Fold herring mixture into the cream. Taste and season with salt and pepper. Garnish with leaf lettuce and lemon wedges if desired. Makes 8 servings.

Savo Beet Salad
Punajuurisalaatti

Carol J. Ristinen
Fergus Falls, Minnesota

1 tablespoon vinegar
1/4 cup heavy cream
1/4 cup mayonnaise
1-1/2 teaspoons horseradish
Dash salt
2 cups cooked beets, diced

Mix together vinegar, cream, mayonnaise, horseradish, and salt. Blend dressing with the beets. Chill. Makes 4 servings.

Old-Fashioned Salad
Vanhanaikainen salaatti

Mrs. Helena Iloniemi, Finland, wife of the former Finnish ambassador to Washington, D.C.

**2 small, fresh heads of Boston
     or bibb lettuce
1/2 European-style cucumber,
     cut into strips**

**Dressing:
1 to 2 hard-cooked eggs
1 teaspoon prepared mustard
1/2 teaspoon salt
1/2 teaspoon sugar or honey
1 tablespoon lemon juice or
     white vinegar
1/2 cup heavy cream, whipped**

Rinse the lettuce well and dry. Chill to crisp. Tear the leaves into pieces and put into salad bowl with the cucumber strips.

To make dressing, separate the hard-cooked egg yolks from the whites. Mash the yolks with the mustard, salt, and sugar or honey. Add lemon juice or vinegar; mix well. Fold in the whipped cream. Chill. Chop the egg white separately. Pour dressing over salad just before serving. Sprinkle with chopped egg white. Serve with meat or fish dishes. Makes 4 to 6 servings.

Vegetable Beef Salad
Vihannes-pihvisalaatti

This is a great way to use leftover cooked beef. It is served as a first course and also as a topping for open-faced sandwiches.

**1/2 cup sugar
2 tablespoons Dijón-style
     mustard
2 teaspoons grated fresh
     onion
Salt to taste
1 small clove garlic, minced
2 tablespoons white wine
     vinegar
1 tablespoon lemon juice
1/2 cup vegetable oil
4 small red potatoes, pared,
     cooked, and cut into
     julienne strips
1 jar (16-ounce) mild pickled
     mixed vegetables, drained
1/2 pound cooked beef, cut
     into julienne strips
Red or green bell pepper rings**

Combine sugar, mustard, onion, salt, garlic, vinegar, and lemon juice in a bowl. With a whisk, blend in the oil until smooth and mixture is blended, making a pale dressing. Combine potatoes, vegetables, and beef with the dressing. Refrigerate at least 3 hours. Garnish with red or green bell pepper rings. Makes 8 servings.

Mushroom Salad

Sienisalaatti

1 pound fresh mushrooms,
    chopped
2 tablespoons finely minced
    onion
2 tablespoons fresh lemon
    juice
1 tablespoon sugar
1/2 teaspoon freshly ground
    pepper
1/2 cup whipping cream
1/4 cup sour cream
1 teaspoon salt
1/8 teaspoon dry mustard
Fresh lettuce to line bowl or
    for garnish

Combine mushrooms, onion, lemon juice, sugar, and pepper in bowl; cover. Refrigerate for 30 minutes to 4 hours. Whip cream until thick; fold in sour cream, salt, and mustard. Stir into mushroom mixture. Turn into serving bowl. If desired, garnish with fresh lettuce leaves. Makes 8 servings.

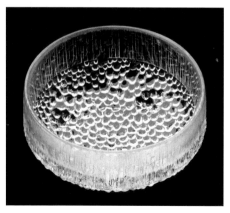

Sour Cream Cucumber Salad

*Kurkkusalaatti
kermakastikkeessa*

This salad should be served in a glass dish and decorated with dill sprigs.

2 European-style cucumbers
    or 4 medium-sized garden
    cucumbers
1 tablespoon salt
1 cup dairy sour cream
1-1/2 tablespoons white vinegar
1/4 cup salad oil
1/2 teaspoon sugar
3 tablespoons chopped fresh
    or dried dill
Salt
Pepper

Scrub cucumbers but do not peel. Cut off ends. Score with tines of fork. Slice **paper thin** (this is very important!). Sprinkle with salt and let stand at room temperature for 1 hour. Drain and rinse to remove salt. Squeeze dry. Combine sour cream, vinegar, salad oil, sugar, and dill. Pour over cucumbers. Add salt and pepper to taste. Chill before serving. Makes 8 servings.

Crystal bowl (icicle design) by Tapio Wirkkala, made by Iittala, world-famous glassmakers of Finland

Photograph courtesy of
Finland National Tourist Office

Salmon Mousse
Lohihyytelö

Soile Anderson
North Oaks, Minnesota

2 pounds salmon meat,
    cooked
2 envelopes unflavored gelatin
1 cup sour cream
2 tablespoons lemon juice
1-1/2 tablespoons prepared
    horseradish
1 teaspoon paprika
1/2 cup diced celery
1/2 cup pimiento-stuffed
    olives, chopped
2 tablespoons finely chopped
    onion
Salt
Fresh dill
Thyme
Black pepper
1/2 cup whipping cream

Drain salmon, reserving liquid. Remove skin and large bones; flake salmon. Add cold water to reserved liquid to equal 1-3/4 cups. In a saucepan, soften gelatin in salmon liquid. Stir over low heat until gelatin is dissolved. Cool slightly. Blend together sour cream, lemon juice, horseradish, and paprika; gradually stir in cooled gelatin mixture. Chill until partially set. Fold in salmon, celery, olives, and onion. Season with salt, fresh dill, thyme, and black pepper to taste. Whip cream just until soft peaks begin to form; fold into mixture. Turn into a 5-1/2-cup fish-shaped mold. Chill until firm. Trim with lettuce.

Mushroom-Stuffed Tomatoes
Tomaatti-sienisalaatti

This is a great garnish around a roast.

8 medium-sized tomatoes
    (they should be perfect)
2 cups finely chopped
    mushrooms
Dash salt
1 cup finely chopped mild
    sweet onion
1 cup cream, whipped
3 tablespoons lemon juice
2 tablespoons prepared mustard
1/2 teaspoon ground white
    pepper
Salt to taste

Cut lids off tomatoes and scoop out seeds and pulp; place upside down on paper toweling to drain. Spread mushrooms over paper toweling and sprinkle lightly with salt; drain 1/2 hour. Combine mushrooms and chopped onion. Blend cream, lemon juice, mustard, and pepper. Add salt if desired. Blend with mushrooms and onions. Fill hollowed-out tomatoes with mushroom mixture. Place lids decoratively on top. Garnish with something green, like parsley or chives. Makes 8 servings.

Finnish Vegetable Dishes

Root vegetables are important to the Finnish diet because they are the ones that are kept throughout the winter. Potatoes, rutabagas, turnips, and carrots are the mainstays. In the summertime, varieties of the cabbage family —red and green cabbage, broccoli, cauliflower, and Brussels sprouts—are grown in home gardens and are abundant in the farmers' market stalls.

Baked Rutabagas
Paistetut lantut

Mrs. Oscar Walsberg
DeKalb, Illinois
This recipe was first included in the Finnish-American Cookbook *compiled by ladies of DeKalb's Bethlehem Evangelical Lutheran Church.*

1 medium-sized rutabaga
1 or 2 eggs, beaten
2 tablespoons Cream of
**   Wheat or farina**
Salt to taste
Enough milk to keep
**   mixture soft**

Pare rutabaga and cut into pieces. Put into pan; cover with water and simmer until rutabaga is tender, 25 to 30 minutes. Drain and mash using electric mixer or potato masher. Add eggs, farina, salt, and milk. Turn into a buttered casserole dish, about 1-1/2 quart capacity. Dot with butter. Bake in a 350°F oven for 30 minutes or until lightly browned.

Rutabaga Casserole
Lanttulaatikko

Irene R. Nelson, McLean, Virginia
Her parents were born in Finland.

2 pounds rutabagas, peeled
**   and cubed**
Water to cover
1/2 cup soft bread crumbs
2 tablespoons melted butter
1 cup cream or milk
1 teaspoon salt
1/2 teaspoon nutmeg
Pepper to taste
1 tablespoon sugar
2 eggs, slightly beaten

Put rutabagas into a saucepan. Cover with water and bring to a boil; lower heat and simmer 25 to 30 minutes or until tender. Drain and mash. Blend in the remaining ingredients. Turn into a buttered 1-1/2 quart-sized baking dish. Place this dish into a larger dish and pour 1-inch hot water in bottom of larger dish. Bake at 350°F for 45 minutes or until a knife inserted in the center comes out clean. Makes 8 servings.

Potato Rutabaga Casserole
Peruna-lanttulaatikko

From old western Finland, this is a favorite combination of Finnish-American people, too! The "sweetening" process is one that is classic to western Finnish cooking. "Because I fear the growth of bacteria, I usually mash the rutabagas and potatoes in the food processor to develop the texture desired, and then cover and refrigerate the mixture overnight. This recipe, however, gives the classic Finnish directions," says Beatrice Ojakangas.

**1 pound rutabagas, pared,
    cut into 1-inch cubes**
**1/2 pound potatoes, pared,
    cut into chunks**
Water to boiling
1/3 cup all-purpose flour
1/2 cup dry bread crumbs
1 cup milk
1/3 cup heavy cream
1/3 cup dark corn syrup
1/4 cup melted butter
2 eggs, beaten
1 teaspoon salt
1/4 teaspoon allspice
1/8 teaspoon white pepper
1/8 teaspoon nutmeg
1/8 teaspoon ginger
Butter

This must be started the day before serving. Boil rutabagas and potatoes in water to cover separately. Drain; reserve cooking liquids. Mash them together. Add flour and about 1/2 cup of the cooking liquid to the mixture. Put into a warm place, cover, and let stand overnight to "sweeten." The next day, soak bread crumbs in milk. Add to the mashed mixture. Add cream, corn syrup, melted butter, eggs, salt, allspice, pepper, nutmeg, and ginger. Mix well. Pour into a buttered shallow 2-quart casserole. Flatten mixture and decorate with back of spoon by making rows of spoon marks. Sprinkle with bread crumbs and dot with butter. Bake 1-1/2 to 2 hours at 300°F. The surface should be golden brown. Makes 8 servings.

Morel Mushroom Sauce
Korvasienikastike

*Soile Anderson
North Oaks, Minnesota*

**1 pound morel mushrooms,
    fresh or frozen**
4 tablespoons butter
2 tablespoons flour
Salt
2 cups sour cream

Boil mushrooms; drain and chop into small pieces. Sauté with butter for 30 minutes at medium heat. Add flour, salt to taste, and sour cream. Continue to cook for 10 minutes. Serve hot with wild game. Also excellent with walleye or salmon.

Creamed Mushrooms

Sienimuhennos

Finns are connoisseurs of wild mushrooms. This is a recipe that can be used for all types of mushrooms and is delicious served over simple boiled new potatoes, poached fresh fish, poached eggs, or with broiled or roasted meats.

4 tablespoons butter
4 cups sliced fresh
**   mushrooms (commercial**
**   or wild)**
1 medium onion, finely
**   chopped**
4 tablespoons flour
1-1/2 cups cream
Salt and pepper to taste

Melt butter in a frying pan and add the mushrooms and onion. Cook over medium heat, stirring constantly until mushrooms and onions are browned and tender. Stir in the flour and the cream. Cook until thickened. Add salt and pepper to taste. Makes about 2-1/2 cups or 6 to 8 servings.

Creamed Radishes

Retiisimuhennos

When radishes get too large to serve raw, use them in this peppery sauce.

10 to 12 large radishes
1/2 teaspoon salt
2 tablespoons butter
2 tablespoons flour
1 cup cream
1/4 teaspoon pepper
2 teaspoons sugar
Chopped parsley

Clean radishes; trim off ends and tips. Place them in a saucepan with enough water to cover, adding 1/2 teaspoon of salt to the water. Cook until tender. Drain but reserve the liquid. Chop and set aside. You should have 2 cups cooked radishes.

In another pan, melt the butter and add the flour, mixing until smooth. Slowly add about 1 cup hot liquid from the radishes, stirring constantly to keep the mixture smooth, then blend in the cream. Add the chopped radishes, pepper, and sugar. Just before serving, heat almost to boiling and garnish with parsley. Serve over carrot or spinach crêpes. Makes 4 to 6 servings.

Carrot Casserole
Porkkanalaatikko

Marlene Luoma
Duluth, Minnesota

1 cup cooked brown or
white rice
2 cups milk
5 large carrots, pared,
shredded
1 teaspoon salt
1 tablespoon dark brown sugar
2 eggs
3 tablespoons butter
1/3 cup fine bread crumbs

Combine rice, milk, carrots, salt, sugar, and eggs. Pour into a buttered 1-quart casserole. Melt butter in a pan and stir in crumbs. Sprinkle over top of casserole. Bake in a 375°F oven for 40 minutes or until top is lightly browned and carrots are cooked (carrots will have a firm texture). Makes 6 servings.

Cauliflower Casserole
Kukkakaalilaatikko

1 small head cauliflower
1/2 cup cooked rice
3 eggs, beaten
1 cup milk
1/2 teaspoon salt
Dash allspice
Fresh chopped parsley

Cook the cauliflower in salted water to cover until tender-crisp (25 to 30 minutes). Separate the flowerets and arrange in a greased casserole. Combine the rice with the eggs, milk, salt, and allspice and pour over the cauliflower. Bake at 350°F for 30 to 35 minutes or until custard has set. Garnish with parsley. Makes 6 servings.

Spinach Pancake
Pinaattipannukakku

This is an oven pancake that is filled and rolled like a jelly roll. Sprinkle shredded cheese over each serving.

2 eggs
2 cups milk
1 cup sifted all-purpose flour
1-1/2 teaspoons salt, divided
1 teaspoon baking powder
4 tablespoons butter, divided
1 pound fresh spinach leaves
1/4 teaspoon nutmeg
Pepper
Shredded Emmenthaler cheese
or Swiss cheese
Sour cream

Beat eggs and milk together. Sift flour with 1 teaspoon salt and baking powder into mixing bowl. Stir in the egg-milk mixture all at once and blend until smooth. Let stand 30 minutes before baking. Melt 1 tablespoon of the butter in a 10 x 15-inch jelly roll pan and spread evenly over the bottom. Pour in the pancake batter. Bake in a 350°F oven for 20 minutes or until set (do not overcook). Meanwhile, cook spinach in a small amount of water until tender; drain thoroughly; add the remaining 3 tablespoons butter, nutmeg, 1/2 teaspoon salt, and pepper to taste. Spread the spinach over the baked pancake and roll up like a jelly roll. Slice and serve hot topped with shredded cheese or sour cream. Makes 6 to 8 servings.

Mashed Potato Casserole
Imelletty perunalaatikko

This old classic casserole is familiar to all Finns. The ingredients are simple enough, but the baking time is long and slow to allow the starch of the potatoes to break down into simple sugars which the Finns call "malting." The resulting dish has a sweet flavor and a yellowish color. This may be baked along with the Karjalan paisti *and served with it as both are baked for many hours.*

3 pounds potatoes, cubed
Water to cover
1/4 cup all-purpose flour
Milk if necessary
Butter
Dark corn syrup (optional)

In water to cover, cook potatoes until tender. Drain, saving the potato water, and mash the potatoes. As you mash the potatoes, add the flour and add some of the cooking water, if needed, to keep the mixture light and fluffy. Turn into a 1-1/2 to 2-quart buttered casserole with a cover. Bake at 250°F for 5 hours, covered. Check occasionally to see that the potatoes do not dry out. Add milk if necessary to keep mixture moist. During this time the potatoes should become yellowish in color and gain a flavor similar to sweet potatoes. Add a pinch or so of salt if desired. After 5 hours, remove from the oven. Remove cover. Dot top with butter and drizzle with dark corn syrup. Increase oven heat to 350°F and bake for 15 minutes or until browned on top. Serve hot. Makes 6 to 8 servings.

Shredded Potato Casserole from Savo
Riivinkropsu

2 eggs
1 cup milk
2 tablespoons all-purpose flour
1 teaspoon salt
6 large potatoes, shredded
2 tablespoons butter
Parsley, chopped

Combine the eggs, milk, flour, and salt with the potatoes. Melt the butter in the bottom of a 1-1/2-quart baking dish and spread evenly over the bottom and sides. Pour in the egg-potato mixture and bake in a 375°F oven for 45 to 50 minutes or until potatoes are tender and the casserole is set. Serve hot garnished with parsley. Makes 6 servings.

Åland Island Potato Cakes
Ahvenanmaan perunakakut

The Åland Islands belong to Finland but have traditions similar to the Swedish. There are many versions of these filled potato cakes throughout all the Scandinavian countries.

1/4 pound bacon, cooked crisp, crumbled, and drained (reserve drippings)
4 large potatoes, pared, cooked, and mashed
1 tablespoon milk
1 egg, slightly beaten
1/2 teaspoon allspice
1/2 teaspoon salt
1 small onion, finely minced

Combine bacon with the potatoes, milk, egg, allspice, salt, and onion until smooth. Shape into patties and fry in the bacon drippings. Serve hot. Makes 4 servings.

Finnish Main Dishes

The main dish for a typical Finnish meal is most often a simmered stew-like dish, a fish dish, or a casserole. Meatless dishes are not uncommon either, as meat is expensive. Fish is reasonable and excellent all over Finland and is most often a freshwater fish. Finnish Americans have carried to America many of the same eating patterns, and the recipes in this section represent a cross section of some of the favorites.

Chilled Veal Loaf
Syltty

Helen Luhtala Johnson
DeKalb, Illinois

1 veal shank or knuckle
2 quarts water (reserve broth)
Salt and pepper to taste
2 or 3 bay leaves
Pinch ground ginger
1/4 cup white vinegar

Place veal in water and bring to a boil. Skim broth; add salt, pepper, and bay leaves; continue cooking until meat is tender. Remove meat and allow to cool. Put meat through food chopper with a coarse blade. Strain broth; add ginger and vinegar. Add more salt and pepper if desired. Pour broth into meat. If there is too much liquid, cook mixture 5 to 10 minutes longer to reduce. Pour mixture into a mold or a loaf pan. Chill overnight. Slice and serve with relishes and condiments at a buffet table.

Delicious Rabbit Casserole

Jänispaisti

Soile Anderson

1 rabbit
1 bottle red wine
Butter
2 onions, chopped
Salt to taste
Black pepper to taste
1 teaspoon thyme
White pepper to taste
1 bunch fresh parsley, chopped
2 cloves garlic
4 cups bouillon
2 tablespoons flour
1 cup heavy cream
1/2 pound fresh mushrooms

Marinate rabbit overnight in red wine; reserve marinade. Cut rabbit into four pieces; dry and sauté in butter until brown. Place rabbit in casserole and add chopped onions, salt, black pepper, thyme, white pepper, chopped parsley, and garlic. Pour bouillon and red wine (from marinade) over rabbit and bake for 1-1/2 hours at low temperature.

Combine flour and heavy cream. Add mixture and mushrooms to casserole. Return to oven and simmer for 15 minutes. This is excellent served with vegetables.

———

Minnesota Iron Range Finns introduced white-tail deer to Finland.

Wild Game (Saddle of Deer)

Riista (peuransatulapaisti)
A Holiday Treat

Soile Anderson
North Oaks, Minnesota

1 deer loin
1 cup port wine
1 cup red wine
2 tablespoons Dijón mustard
1 cup cognac
2 tablespoons salt
2 tablespoons freshly ground
   black pepper
Bacon
Cornstarch
Parsley, finely chopped

Combine port wine, red wine, Dijón mustard, cognac, salt, and pepper. Marinate deer loin in mixture for 24 hours, turning a few times. Remove loin from marinade and wipe dry, saving marinade. Wrap loin in bacon, place in oven, and brown at 400°F for 15 minutes. Pour marinade over meat and reduce temperature to 300°F. Bake until meat is medium (pink center). Remove meat from oven, saving liquid.

To make a sauce, thicken cooking liquid with 2 tablespoons cornstarch per quart of liquid. Slowly bring sauce to a boil and simmer for 10 minutes. Add finely chopped parsley and season to taste.

Christmas Ham with Prunes

Joulukinkku

1 fresh ham (pork leg), 6 to 8
    pounds
20 pitted prunes, coarsely
    chopped
1 cup minced onion
1-1/2 cups pared, chopped
    apple
1/4 cup applesauce
1 (10-1/2-ounce) can beef
    consommé
1 cup currant jelly
1/2 cup orange juice
1/3 cup port wine
1/2 teaspoon salt

Have butcher remove center bone from a fresh pork leg and cut a deep pocket in the cavity. Combine prunes with onion, apples, and applesauce. Stuff ham with apple mixture; overlap and secure ends. Tie with string to keep together. Score fat side of ham; place ham with fat side up on a bed of onions in a shallow baking pan. Pour consommé over ham. Roast at 325°F for 30 to 35 minutes per pound or to 170°F on meat thermometer, basting often with pan juices. Transfer ham to serving platter and keep warm. Remove and discard fat from pan juices. Bring juices to a boil, stirring in browned bits clinging to bottom and sides of pan.

Boil to reduce juices, about 5 minutes. Stir in currant jelly, orange juice, port wine, and salt; simmer 10 to 15 minutes. To serve, remove string from ham; slice thinly. Serve sauce in gravy boat or sauce dish; pour sauce over ham. Makes 6 to 8 servings.

Finnish Simmered Lamb

Lammasmuhennos

Donald Peryam, Hancock, Michigan

2-1/2 pounds lean lamb shoulder
6 medium potatoes, pared
    and cubed
4 medium carrots, pared and cut
    into 1-inch pieces
2 medium onions, peeled and
    cut into eighths
1-1/2 teaspoons salt
1/4 teaspoon pepper
2 to 3 cups water
2 to 3 tablespoons chopped
    parsley
6 to 7 whole allspice

In a heavy roaster or Dutch oven, make a layer of the lamb. Top lamb with the potatoes, carrots, and onions; sprinkle with salt and pepper, then add the water. Add parsley and allspice. Cover and simmer slowly for 1-1/2 to 2 hours until meat is very tender, or bake in a 350°F oven for 1-1/2 to 2 hours. Makes 6 to 10 servings.

Finnish Meatballs
Lihapyörykät

Meatballs are a favorite in Finland and always right for guest meals, or for the voileipäpöytä. Serve them with lingonberries or cranberry sauce, sliced beets, pickles, lanttulaatikko, and mashed potatoes.

3/4 cup soft bread crumbs
1 cup light cream or milk,
 divided
1-1/2 pounds lean ground beef
1 onion, minced
1 egg, slightly beaten
1-1/2 teaspoons salt
1/2 teaspoon ground allspice
2 tablespoons butter for frying
2 tablespoons flour
1-1/2 cups milk

Soak bread crumbs in 1/2 cup of the cream. Blend in the beef, onion, egg, salt, and allspice. Shape into balls about 1 inch in diameter. Melt butter in skillet and brown the meatballs a few at a time. Shake pan to roll meatballs around so they brown evenly. After all the meat is browned, remove from pan; add flour to drippings; stir and brown over medium heat. Slowly add the second half-cup of cream and the milk, stirring to keep mixture smooth. Add water if necessary to thin out the gravy. Strain if necessary. Return meatballs to pan, cover, and simmer 25 minutes over low heat. Makes 6 servings.

Cabbage Rolls
Kaalikääryleet

Mrs. Ted (Esther) Luoma, Duluth, Minnesota, is the mother of Beatrice Ojakangas. Esther's cabbage rolls can be made ahead and frozen if desired—so handy when you have a busy schedule. Esther, mother of ten children, is remembered for her grand entertainment of family and delicious feasts on birthdays and holidays. Going to "Grandma's and Grandpa's" has special memories for all thirty-two grandchildren!

1/2 cup medium-grain rice
1-1/4 cups milk
1 large head cabbage
1 pound ground beef
1/4 pound ground pork
1 cup milk
2 teaspoons salt
1/4 teaspoon pepper
Fat for browning rolls
2 tablespoons brown sugar
1/2 cup hot water

Cook the rice in the 1-1/4 cups milk until tender. Remove cabbage leaves from head and immerse in boiling salted water until leaves are pliable. Drain. Combine ground beef and pork with the 1 cup milk, salt and pepper, and cooked rice. Mix well. Spoon meat mixture onto each leaf, roll, and tie or fasten with toothpicks. Heat fat in a heavy skillet and brown the cabbage rolls slowly, turning to brown all sides. Sprinkle with the brown sugar and add the water. Cover and simmer slowly about 1 hour or until rolls are cooked through. Thicken the broth to make a gravy. Makes 6 servings.

Meat and Cabbage Casserole
Liha-kaalilaatikko

This casserole combines the favorite flavors of cabbage rolls but with much less effort. Serve with lingonberries and potatoes.

1 small head cabbage, shredded
2 tablespoons butter
2 tablespoons dark corn syrup
2 teaspoons salt
1/4 teaspoon ground marjoram
1 pound lean ground beef
1 cup soft bread crumbs
1/2 cup milk
2 eggs, beaten

Put cabbage into deep pot and add enough boiling water to cover; simmer 5 minutes until tender-crisp; drain. Add butter, syrup, salt, and marjoram. In another bowl, mix the ground beef, bread crumbs, milk, and eggs. Butter a 2- to 2-1/2-quart casserole and layer the cabbage and meat mixture, beginning and ending with the cabbage. Bake at 350°F for 1 hour or until casserole is browned and meat is done. Makes 6 to 8 servings.

Cabbage Pie
Kaalipiirakka

Mrs. Helena Iloniemi, Finland

Crust:
2 cups unbleached all-purpose flour
1 teaspoon salt
3 sticks unsalted butter
1 tablespoon cognac
1/2 cup heavy cream
1 egg, lightly beaten

Filling:
4 pounds cabbage, center removed, cut in half
Water
1-1/2 tablespoons salt
1/2 to 3/4 stick unsalted butter
4 tablespoons corn syrup or molasses
1-1/2 to 2 teaspoons salt
1/8 teaspoon white pepper
1 tablespoon white vinegar

To make the crust, combine flour and salt; cut in butter until grains are the size of small peas. Add cognac, cream, and lightly beaten egg, mixing quickly. Make a ball of dough. Chill 1 hour.

Cook cabbage in salted water to cover. Chill. Chop coarsely. Divide butter between two large, heavy iron frying pans. Brown the cooked cabbage slowly to bring out the delicious flavor. At first, keep the heat moderately low, and let cabbage lose some liquid. Stir once in a while.

When the cabbage has shrunk, increase the heat. Now the cabbage should be browned evenly—not just golden but nicely brown. When the cabbage is brown, add the corn syrup or molasses, salt, pepper, and vinegar. Stir well. Remove from pan and cool.

Preheat oven to 425°F. Divide the dough into two parts. On a floured board, roll out the bottom crust to the size of a baking sheet. The crust should be thin. Put the crust on a lightly greased baking sheet or pan. Spoon the cabbage onto the crust leaving about 1-1/2 inches empty at the sides. The finished pie will be about 1 inch thick. Roll out the top crust; place on top of the filling and seal the edges well; turn up and seal again. Brush with egg and prick with a fork. Bake about 30 to 40 minutes. Serve as a lunch dish, snack, sandwich, or appetizer. It is good warm or cold. Spread lightly with butter, if you want to indulge. (In Finland, cabbage pie with a glass of milk or beer is a favorite after-sauna food.) Makes 8 to 10 servings.

Poronliha (reindeer meat) is very lean, fine-grained, and tender. Prepared in many ways, it is most often served with fruit or a fruit sauce. It is also dried and smoked.

Spinach and Carrot Crêpes
Pinaatti-porkkanaräiskäleet

Räiskaleet is an old Finnish word for thin pancakes. With a mushroom filling, these crêpe-like pancakes turn into a wonderful meatless main dish!

6 eggs
1 cup rye flour
2 cups milk
2 teaspoons salt
2 teaspoons sugar
4 ounces fresh spinach leaves (from 8-ounce bunch with stalks on)
1-1/2 cups shredded fresh carrot
Butter for cooking and brushing filled crêpes
Mushroom filling and sauce (recipe follows)

In a large bowl, mix the eggs, flour, milk, salt, and sugar until smooth; let stand 30 minutes. Divide into two equal parts. Wash spinach and dry thoroughly. Chop fine. Add to half the crêpe mixture. Add carrots to the second half of the mixture. Working with one batch at a time, bake crêpes in buttered 6-inch crêpe pan using 1/4 cup of the mixture for each. Tilt pan to spread batter evenly. When lightly browned on one side and top looks "set," turn over and cook just a few seconds. Continue cooking both varieties of crêpes, stacking them one on top of the other. You should have two stacks of crêpes, one spinach and one carrot. There will be about 10 of each variety. Serve them just buttered or fill them with the mushroom filling, rolling them so that the browned side is on the inside of each crêpe. Place them side by side on a buttered ovenproof platter. Brush with butter and heat at 400°F for 10 to 15 minutes until hot. Serve with sour cream or mushroom sauce and lingonberries.

Mushroom Filling and Sauce: In a wide frying pan melt 1/4 cup butter; add 1 small onion, chopped, and 2 pounds sliced fresh mushrooms. Simmer until mushroom liquid is gone. Remove 2 cups of the mushrooms. Add 2 cups cooked brown rice. Season to taste. Use this filling for the crêpes.

To make the sauce, add 1 cup beef consommé and 1/2 cup whipping cream to the reserved mushrooms. Boil until thickened and reduced to about 2 cups.

The Bear
Finland national nature symbol

Salt Pork Stew With Raisin Dumplings
Läskisoosi ja rusinaklimpit

Ellen M. Johnson
Eveleth, Minnesota
Ellen says, "My parents and grandfather immigrated here from Finland in the early 1900s. My mother used to make this stew as a main dish in my childhood. I was married in 1934 and continued making it during the depression years. Now I make it as a gourmet treat! I'm a homemaker, mother of three, grandmother of eight, and a great-grandmother." Ellen suggests serving this dish with homemade whole grain bread and cheese.

1-1/2 cups diced salt pork
1 medium onion, chopped
5 cups water
5 whole allspice
1 heaping cup sliced carrots or
half rutabagas and
half carrots
2-1/4 cups coarsely cut
potatoes

Klimppi:
1/4 cup milk
1 egg, slightly beaten
1 cup flour
1/8 teaspoon salt
Dash of pepper
1/2 cup raisins

Soak salt pork in boiling water to cover for 1/2 hour; drain. Put salt pork into heavy Dutch oven and sauté over medium heat until golden brown. Drain fat, leaving about 2 tablespoons in the pan. Add chopped onion; brown lightly. Add water and allspice. Cook at low boil for 15 minutes, covered. Add carrots; cook 15 minutes; add potatoes and cook until almost done, about 20 to 25 minutes. Add water to keep broth from evaporating too much. Keep covered while cooking. Taste for salt. Usually no salt is needed as salt pork is quite salty.

For *klimpit*: Mix milk and egg. Add flour, salt, and pepper and beat well. Add raisins and mix well. Drop by teaspoonfuls on bubbling stew. Cook, covered, for 15 minutes.

Pork Chops With Mustard Sauce

Porsaankyljykset sinappikastikkeessa

Nino de Prado, Finnish Tourist Board, New York, New York
Serve this with boiled potatoes, green vegetables, and a salad.

4 pork chops
French or spicy mustard
1/2 pint heavy cream
1 to 2 bouillon cubes
    (optional)
Salt and pepper

Use 1 thick, lean pork chop per person. Place in a hot frying pan or iron skillet. Cover each chop on both sides with a generous amount of strong mustard. Brown chops on both sides until golden brown, cover, reduce heat, and cook for an additional 5 minutes or until done. Remove chops and keep warm. Add heavy cream to pan and stir into scrapings to make sauce. For additional flavor, add 1 bouillon cube to the sauce. Let simmer until the color of the sauce is light brown. Add extra mustard, salt, and pepper to flavor sauce. Then place pork chops in sauce and simmer for an additional 5 minutes. Makes 4 servings.

Beef or Venison Sami Stir-Fry

Gerry Kangas, Aurora, Minnesota
Gerry says her grandmother used to prepare this dish using frozen venison, and would sometimes thicken the liquid with a flour paste to make a gravy. She recalls a delicious, gourmet meal, at the Sky Hotel in Rovaniemi, of shaved reindeer served over mashed potatoes, root vegetables, lingonberries, and a choice of blueberry brule or cloudberries with squeaky cheese.

1 piece of frozen venison or beef
Shortening for browning
Salt to taste
Chopped onion (optional)

Thaw frozen venison or beef slowly. While still partially frozen, cutting

132–

across the grain, shave thin slices into a strainer to drain liquid from meat. Melt shortening in a skillet and brown the meat quickly, turning frequently so it doesn't get hard. Season with salt and add the chopped onion if desired. When the onion is cooked through, add water to cover the meat. Partially cover the skillet and cook on low heat until done.

North Country Pasties
Lihapiiraat

Lois Raati Mattson, Esko, Minnesota Pasties have come to be known as a Finnish food, even though internationally they are associated with the Cornish people. Pasties were a lunchbox favorite of the miners.

Pastry:
3 cups flour
1-1/2 teaspoons salt
1 teaspoon baking powder
1 cup lard
1 egg
1 tablespoon vinegar
Ice cold water

Filling:
6 small potatoes, pared and diced
1 cup diced celery
1 cup diced carrots
1/4 cup minced onion
2 teaspoons salt
Dash pepper
3 pounds ground raw beef or diced beef round steak

Mix flour, salt, and baking powder. Cut in lard until the mixture resembles coarse crumbs. Combine egg, vinegar, and 3 tablespoons ice water; sprinkle over flour mixture; blend. Add cold water until mixture holds together in a ball. Roll six ovals out to the size of a dinner plate. Combine filling ingredients. Mound 1/6 of the filling on one half of each round of dough. Dot tops with butter. Fold other half of dough over. Seal edges. Bake at 400°F 20 minutes, reduce temperature to 350°F, and bake 20 minutes longer. Brush top with butter before serving. Makes 6 pasties.

Karelian Three-Meat Stew
Karjalanpaisti

1 pound beef for stew, cut into 1-inch cubes
1 pound lamb for stew, cut into 1-inch cubes
1 pound boneless pork, cut into 1-inch cubes
5 medium-sized onions, sliced
1 tablespoon salt
1 teaspoon ground allspice
1 to 2 bay leaves

In a large, heavy casserole with a lid, layer the meats with the onion, salt, and allspice. Top with the bay leaves. Cover tightly and bake at 275°F for 5 hours. Meat will be very tender and will stew in its own juice. It is not necessary to add other broth or juice unless the dish is not well covered, and it cooks dry. Remove bay leaves before serving. Thin broth is traditionally not thickened. *Karjalanpaisti* is usually served with boiled new potatoes. Makes 8 to 10 servings.

Poached Fillet of Perch in Dill
Keitetty tilliahven

Nino de Prado, Finnish Tourist Board, New York, New York
Nino says, "Despite my Spanish-sounding name I am a bona fide third-generation Finn." This method may be used to cook any other sweet or freshwater fish. Serve with boiled potatoes and a green salad.

1 to 2 small fillets of fish
  per person
1 to 2 tablespoons butter
Fresh dill, finely chopped
Salt and pepper

In an iron casserole or heavy pot, melt butter; place fillets to cover bottom of pot. Sprinkle liberally with fresh dill; season lightly with salt and pepper. Place a new layer of fillets on top. Repeat by sprinkling dill and seasoning, until four or five layers have been built. Cover tightly, and simmer on low heat for about 10 to 15 minutes. Don't overcook. The natural juices from the fish provide a succulent sauce for the delicious tasting fish.

Fish Pie
Kalapiiras

Mrs. Helena Iloniemi, Finland

Potato pastry shell:
1-1/2 cups unbleached
  all-purpose flour
1 teaspoon salt
1-1/2 cups butter or margarine
1-1/2 cups cooked and mashed
  potatoes
Beaten egg for brushing

Filling:
1/3 cup rice
1 cup fish stock or water
2-1/4 pounds filleted smelts
  or herring
4 eggs, hard-cooked, chopped
2 bunches fresh dill, chopped
3 teaspoons salt
1 teaspoon white pepper
1/4 cup (1/2 stick) butter, melted

To prepare pastry, combine flour and salt in a bowl. Cut in the butter until mixture resembles coarse crumbs. Add mashed potatoes and

134–

blend just until dough holds together in a ball. Chill 30 minutes. Cook the rice in the fish stock or water.

Divide pastry into two parts. Roll out one part to fit the bottom of a 10-inch pie pan or 2-quart shallow baking dish. Layer rice, fish fillets, chopped eggs, dill, salt, and pepper in the pastry-lined dish. Drizzle with the melted butter. Roll out second part of pastry and cover filling. Pinch edges together to seal pastry. Prick with a fork to make vent holes. Brush with beaten egg.

Bake at 350°F for 1 to 1-1/2 hours. Serve as it is or with dill-flavored melted butter. Makes 8 to 10 servings.

Finnish Fish Chowder
Kalakeitto

Natalie Saari Gallagher, St. Paul
"This fish chowder," says Natalie, "is called mojakka by Finnish-Americans. In Finland the word is foreign, and there is much speculation as to how it came to be a Finnish-American name for this soup. But by any name, and made with almost any fish, mojakka is pronounced 'delicious'!" The recipe works well with almost any fish, even those that are difficult to fillet, because the bones can be "lifted out" after the fish is pre-cooked and cooled slightly. Natalie remembers her dad making this over the campfire on the shore of Lake Vermilion. Makes 4 to 6 servings.

4 small or 2 medium-sized fish
1-1/2 teaspoons salt
12 small new potatoes or
    1 pound potatoes, pared and quartered
1 medium-sized onion, sliced
1/8 teaspoon white pepper
3 whole allspice (optional)
3 tablespoons butter
1-1/2 cups milk
1 tablespoon flour mixed
    with 1/4 cup cold water

Clean the fish; remove heads, tails, and fins. Place whole fish in large pot, adding just enough boiling water to cover the fish (about 2 cups). Add salt and cook for 15 minutes or until fish takes on an opaque appearance and is done. Lift out the fish to a large platter, leaving the liquid in the cooking pot. Add the potatoes to this liquid and cook until tender; add sliced onion, pepper, and allspice. While potatoes are cooking, separate the fish into large (bite-sized) pieces as you lift out the backbone and other bones from the fish. Add the fish pieces, butter, milk, and flour mixture to

The lion is a symbol of Finland.

–135

the potatoes and liquid in the pot. Cook until mixture resumes boiling. Serve immediately in large soup bowls. Fresh bread as an accompaniment makes this a whole meal.

St. Urho's Day Fish Stew
Pyhä Urhon mojakka

This stew is included in the St. Urho's Day Menu on page 158.

6 large potatoes, pared and cut into chunks
1 large onion, diced
2 teaspoons salt
5 whole allspice
6 cups water
3 pounds cleaned freshwater fish (i.e., trout, walleye, whitefish)
2 cups cream or 1 (13-ounce) can undiluted evaporated milk
2 tablespoons butter
Dill to taste

Into large soup kettle put potatoes, onion, salt, allspice, and water. Cover and bring to a boil. Simmer 15 to 20 minutes until potatoes are tender. Cut fish into 2-inch chunks. Lower fish into pot with the potatoes; cover and simmer 15 minutes until fish flakes when probed with a fork. Stew should not boil; fish should remain in rather large pieces (if overcooked it falls apart). Add cream, butter, and dill weed if desired. Serve hot. Makes 6 servings.

Fish Casserole
Kalalaatikko

Mrs. Helena Iloniemi, Finland
This is served as a lunch or dinner dish with potatoes and/or bread and a light green salad.

3/4 to 1 pound cleaned small smelts
1/8 teaspoon white pepper
3/4 to 1 cup heavy cream
1 (2-ounce) can Swedish anchovies (Boviks)
1 teaspoon butter or oil
2 tablespoons chopped dill

Preheat oven to 400°F. Remove the backbones from the smelts. Grease a shallow flameproof dish and place fish in it, tightly side by side. Sprinkle with pepper. Mix cream and chopped anchovies; spoon over the fish. Dot lightly with butter or sprinkle with oil. Bake about 20 minutes. The surface of the dish should be a little dry and browned. Sprinkle with dill. Makes 4 servings.

Finnish Salmon Pie
Lohipiirakka

This is a flaky-crusted pie or coulibiac *that is filled with fish. Salmon is the original filling, but our Lake Superior trout is excellent. If you fish, use fresh caught fish of any kind (providing it isn't full of bones).*

Cottage cheese pastry:
1-1/2 cups all-purpose flour
3/4 cup (1-1/2 sticks) unsalted butter, firm
3/4 cup small curd cottage cheese
1 to 2 tablespoons ice water, if necessary

Filling:
1 (3-pound) fillet of Lake Superior trout, skinned
1/4 cup butter
Juice of 1/2 lemon
1/2 teaspoon salt
1/4 cup dry white wine
3/4 cup cooked, salted rice
2 hard-cooked eggs, peeled, sliced
1/2 teaspoon dill weed
1/4 teaspoon white pepper

Glaze:
1 egg
2 tablespoons milk

To prepare pastry, fit food processor with steel blade and measure flour into work bowl. Slice butter and drop into bowl with flour; add cottage cheese. Process using on/off pulses until pastry forms; add ice water if necessary. To prepare without food processor, measure flour into bowl and cut in butter in pea-sized pieces. Add the cottage cheese and blend with fork until pastry is stiff and evenly blended. Chill 30 minutes.

To prepare filling, cut fish into 5-inch pieces for easier handling. Heat butter in large skillet over high heat. Brown fish pieces in two batches using the same pan. Brown just until golden, but not until cooked through or fish will be dry and overcooked after baking in crust. Sprinkle both sides with lemon juice and salt. Remove fish from pan and hold on plate as you finish browning the remaining pieces. Cool to room temperature. Strain butter from pan; reserve. Add wine to pan and over high heat, scrape up the brownings. Boil down to about 2 tablespoons and strain into the cooked rice. Mix until blended.

Line a large baking sheet with parchment paper. Divide pastry into two parts. Roll each half into a rectangle 12 x 6 inches. Place half of the pastry onto parchment paper. Sprinkle pastry with flour and top with half of the pre-browned fish. Leave 1 to 1-1/2 inches of pastry uncovered around the edges. Top fish with the rice, then with a layer of hard-cooked eggs; sprinkle with dill and white pepper. Top with remaining fish. Drizzle the reserved butter from frying pan over fish. Fold pastry up to make a 1-inch edge around the filling of fish. Mix egg and milk for glaze and paint outside of the standing edge with the mixture.

Roll out second half of the pastry and trim to make a 12 x 6-inch rectangle. Lay pastry over pie to enclose filling and press around edges to seal. (Pastry will cover the upturned 1-inch edge so that it will be a double layer around the edge. This will give it extra support while baking.) Brush surface with egg glaze. Roll out trimmings, brush with glaze, then cut into strips and place decoratively over the top crust. With tip of knife, make three small vent holes evenly spaced over the top of the pie. Bake at 375°F for 35 to 40 minutes or until pastry is golden. Serve warm; cut crosswise into slices. If desired, serve with sour cream as a sauce to spoon over individual servings. Extra slices of lemon are nice, too. Makes about 8 servings.

———————————

Saints alive!
According to a "corruption index," Finland is the least corrupt country in the world, followed closely by Denmark and New Zealand, respectively.

Aimo's Smoked Fish

Aimo Tervakoski
Silver Spring, Maryland
You'll need some special equipment for smoking fish. Aimo says it's simple to make a fish smoker and your fish will taste better because you did it yourself.

Fish (salmon, herring, lake trout, or whitefish)
Finnish fish smoker
Salt
Water
Wood chips (apple, hickory, or elder wood)

Fish Smoker:
One 6-quart cast iron pot with air-tight cover. A wire net of galvanized or stainless steel 1-1/6 inch or thicker. One metal can 1-1/2 inches tall. This is a small smoker.

Prepare fish:
Remove heads and insides, leaving scale and skin intact. Cut large fish into pieces. Mix 1/4 cup salt to 1 gallon water. Pour over fish and soak for 8 hours in covered container.

Start a fire. Fill can with 1/4 inch of water and place in bottom of cast iron pot. (If you are using a greasy fish such as salmon or herring, add no water as they are moist enough.) Place the wood chips around the can in a 1-inch layer to cover bottom of pot. Place wire netting on top of can and lay the salted fish in a single layer on the net.

Cover tightly and place over fire.

Smoking time varies with size of fish and temperature of fire. Small fish will take 30 to 45 minutes, while large fish may smoke for up to 2 hours. A fully smoked fish will be a rich brown color. When ready, remove pot from fire and take fish off wire rack.

Serve hot or cold. Fish keep for one week when refrigerated. Serve with cold beer or a cool drink made with Finlandia vodka.

Salmon Casserole
Lohilaatikko

This is known by the old name of laksloda *to many Finnish Americans.*

4 medium-sized potatoes
1 can (16-ounce) pink or red salmon, skin and bones removed
1 small onion, thinly sliced
2 tablespoons flour
Milk
2 tablespoons butter

Pare and slice the potatoes. Butter a 1-1/2-quart casserole and place half the potatoes in the bottom of the casserole. Top with the fish and onion. Sprinkle with flour. Add remaining potatoes. Pour enough milk over to cover the potatoes. Dot with butter and bake at 350°F for about 1 hour or until slightly browned and potatoes are tender. Makes 4 servings.

Swan
Finland national nature symbol
(A symbol of the swan is used often to designate environmentally safe products.)

Finnish Homemade Cheese

Finnish homemade cheeses are delicious. In years past, the cheeses were made with the first milk after a cow freshened. Later, flat baked cheese, which was often called "squeaky cheese," was thickened with rennet and baked. Finnish-American cooks also made the same cheeses, more so in the past than today.

Finnish homemade cheeses are most easily made with unhomogenized milk, which is difficult to get unless you own a cow. Regular milk, pasteurized and homogenized, does work, and we have included two recipes in this book. The time that it takes for milk to coagulate after the addition of rennet and the amount of rennet needed is greater with homogenized milk.

A favorite cultured milk is called *viili*. People often ask for a recipe. It is necessary to have a "seed" or "start" for *viili* in order to make it. *Viili* is something like yogurt in that it depends on bacterial action to set milk. The bacteria are different than in yogurt, providing a smoother texture. The best way to make *viili* is to find a Finn who has a starter, and then ask that Finn for directions!

Finnish Squeaky Cheese

Leipäjuusto

Lilya White, Aurora, Minnesota
Lilya demonstrated cheese making at the Smithsonian's 1980 American Folklife Festival in Washington, D.C. Lilya left Finland in 1948. She demonstrates flax and wool spinning at ethnic fairs and also fashions wooden kitchen utensils. She uses the mäntä *utensil in her cheese making.*

3 gallons milk
1/4 of a rennet tablet
2 tablespoons salt

Heat milk to just 100°F. Dissolve the rennet in a tablespoon of water and add it and the salt to the warmed milk. Stir together. Cover with a towel and let set for at least an hour when the mixture starts to form curds. Do not stir or touch during this time. After the hour or so when the curd has jelled, it can be tested by placing a spoon in the center to see whether a hole is left when removing the spoon. Pour the mass that forms onto the center of a large towel that has been draped over a pail or large dishpan and bring the corners of the towel together to make a bag. Let drain and keep squeezing and shaping the mass until it is fairly dry. Never touch the cheese with your hand, only with the outside of the towel. Place one hand underneath; open the towel and invert onto an ungreased pizza pan. Let set again and drain and discard the whey that separates from the cheese. Sprinkle salt on the cheese and place under broiler. Have another pizza pan available so that the cheese can be flipped over onto the other pan. Again, sprinkle salt on top side and return to the broiler for another 15 minutes. It should be watched very closely to avoid over-browning and burning. Keep the pail or dishpan close by so that you can keep draining and discarding the whey that keeps separating from the cheese. Again, remember not to touch the cheese with your hands. When lightly browned, remove from the oven again, draining off the whey. Let cool.

Buttermilk Cheese
Piimäjuusto

Freshly made cheese is a popular dessert in Finland when served with berries. It is often served on the voileipäpöytä *(smorgasbord).*

2 eggs
1 quart cultured buttermilk
3 quarts skim milk
Salt
Sugar

Beat the eggs and the buttermilk together with a whisk. Put milk into a pot and heat to 175°F to 190°F. Gradually pour the mixture of buttermilk and eggs into the hot milk, stirring well the whole time. Keep the temperature of the milk at 180°F until the mixture curdles. When whey has separated, strain the whole mixture through a fine sieve or cheesecloth into a bowl. Add salt and a pinch of sugar to the cheese curd. Line a cheese mold with dampened cheesecloth or muslin and ladle in the curd. Fold over the corners of the cloth and press the cheese gently. Chill under a weight for 4 hours to overnight.

Finnish-Swiss Cheese

Finnish-Swiss cheese is exported worldwide and is as well known as Switzerland's cheese. Finnish-Swiss cheese cures for more than a 100 days compared to a typical 60-day curing time for other European Swiss cheeses.

Lappi Cheese

Lappi *is a semisoft, semisweet cheese that slices easily and is excellent in recipes that call for melting. It comes from Finland's Lapland region.*

Turunmaa

Turunmaa *is a mild, very creamy, natural semisoft cheese with small holes, similar to Danish Cream Havarti. It is both a table cheese and a breakfast cheese to be served with fruit and bread.*

Finnish Desserts

Desserts after a typical Finnish dinner are usually a fruit or rice pudding and are light. Fruit soups made with wild berries are served in the summertime with a drizzle of cream or milk, and in the wintertime the soup is a "sauce" served over rice pudding.

Pies, tortes, cakes, and cookies are usually saved for the "coffee table," which is the favorite Finnish way to entertain. A suggested menu for the Finnish coffee table appears on page 158. It is generally served in three courses. With the first course, the coffee table participant takes a piece of cardamom-flavored white bread and a cup of coffee. The second course is a piece of un-iced cake. The third course is the fancy filled cake. All along, a selection of cookies rounds out the menu. A full-fledged coffee table menu will have seven different items on it.

Finnish Air Pudding
Ilmapuuro

Olga Park, Virginia, Minnesota
This cranberry dessert was made in the homes of wealthy people where Olga worked as a very young girl. Wild cranberries were a staple of the Finns. They were a good source of vitamins in the long winter. Her parents picked large containers of cranberries in the fall, letting them freeze in a shed in the winter. They took them out as they were needed. Her dad mashed a bowlful, and added sugar and rye flour to thicken. They all loved this treat! This dessert is known by more than one name. For example, Ilmapuuro *translates to "air pudding;"* Vispipuuro *translates to "whipped pudding."*

2 cups fresh cranberries
3 cups water
1 cup sugar, more or less, according to taste
1/3 cup farina

Put cranberries and water into saucepan and boil cranberries until all are popped and juice is a nice red color. Strain, reserving juice. Add sugar and farina and cook over low heat until farina has thickened the mixture. Stir to keep from sticking to bottom of pan, about 15 minutes. Pour into large bowl or leave in pan if it is a type that will withstand beaters. Cool to room temperature. Place bowl in pan of cold water and beat with electric beaters until pink and fluffy, changing water as it warms, about 15 to 25 minutes. Serve plain with a dollop of whipped cream, or with half-and-half poured over the top.

Cranberry Sauce
Karpalokeitto

Ellen Maki, Aurora, Minnesota
This is delicious served over creamy rice pudding.

1 package (16-ounce) cranberries
3-1/2 cups water
2-1/2 cups granulated sugar
2-1/2 tablespoons cornstarch
1/4 cup water

In large, 3-quart pot, bring cranberries, water, and sugar to a boil. Cover and let simmer for 15 minutes. Mix cornstarch with 1/4 cup water. Add to sauce while stirring. Boil for 1 minute. Strain sauce. Cool and serve as dessert. Makes 1-1/2 quarts, or 6 to 8 servings.

Golden Sauce
Kultavelli

Mrs. Ethel Saari Wuori
Elk River, Minnesota
This recipe was given to Ethel Wuori by her mother-in-law, Mary Wuori. A "sauce" to Finnish Americans is always a dessert. Others might call it a fruit soup.

1/4 cup medium-grain rice
1 package (12- to 16-ounce)
    pitted prunes
1-1/2 cups raisins
1 quart water
1 cinnamon stick

1 cup sugar
2 tablespoons cornstarch
1/2 cup cold water
1 tablespoon butter
2 tablespoons vinegar

Combine rice, prunes, raisins, water, cinnamon stick, and sugar in a large pot. Simmer slowly until fruits are very tender and rice is cooked, about 1 hour.

Combine cornstarch and 1/2 cup cold water and stir into the boiling sauce. When mixture is thickened, top with the butter and add the vinegar. Serve warm or chilled.

Light and Airy Torte
Tuuleman torttu

Ritva Kamrin, Haslett, Michigan

2 eggs
2 cups sugar
1-1/2 sticks (3/4 cup) melted
    butter or margarine
1 cup milk
3 cups all-purpose flour
2 teaspoons baking powder
2 teaspoons vanilla sugar

Frosting:
1-1/4 cups powdered sugar
4 tablespoons melted butter
4 tablespoons cold coffee
1 tablespoon cocoa or
    chocolate syrup
Coconut flakes

Beat eggs and sugar until creamy. Add butter. Combine flour, baking powder, and vanilla sugar and add to the creamed mixture alternately with the milk. Mix until smooth. Pour batter into a greased 11 x 17 x 1-inch pan. Bake at 350°F for 25 to 30 minutes until cake tests done.

To mix frosting, combine frosting ingredients and beat until smooth. Spread over cake while cake is warm. Top with coconut. Cut into squares and serve.

Creamy Oven Rice Pudding
Riisipuuro

Sylvia Hokkanen
Aurora, Minnesota
Finns often serve baked rice pudding with a berry sauce or fruit soup spooned over the top. Popular as a Christmas dish, it is also great as a simple Sunday night supper!

3/4 cup white long-grained rice
1 quart whole milk
1/2 to 1 teaspoon salt
1 tablespoon sugar

Put rice into a 1-1/2-quart baking dish. Cover with milk; add the salt and sugar. Cover and bake at 350°F for about 1 hour or until rice is tender. Do not stir more than 3 times during baking. If rice starts to dry out during baking, add a little more milk to keep it creamy. Makes 6 servings.

Fruit Soup
Sekahedelmäkeitto

Donald Peryam
Hancock, Michigan
When in season, add fresh raspberries or blueberries to this recipe.

1-1/2 pounds mixed dried
fruit (apricots, prunes,
pears, apples, raisins)
2-3/4 quarts (11 cups) water
1 cinnamon stick
1-1/2 cups white sugar
2 tablespoons cornstarch
2 tablespoons cold water

Simmer the dried fruits in the water with the cinnamon stick and sugar until fruit is tender, about 1/2 to 1 hour. Mix the cornstarch in the 2 tablespoons water. Bring soup to a boil and stir in the cornstarch mixture. Pour this mixture into the fruit pot and simmer again until thick. Can be served cold or hot with cream or whipped cream.

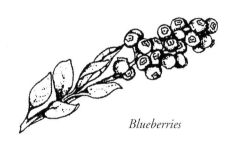

Blueberries

Strawberry Sauce
Mansikkakiisseli

*Gerry Kangas, Aurora, Minnesota
Gerry notes that* kiisseli *is an Eastern
Finland-Russian term that usually
refers to a very thick sauce, but says
they once had a Finnish cook that
called all berry sauces* kiisseli.

**1 pint fresh small strawberries
1 cup water, divided
1-1/2 tablespoons sugar
1 tablespoon potato starch**

Wash and remove stems from the
ripest berries (about half) and put in
a bowl. Place remaining half in a
saucepan, cover with 3/4 cup water,
and bring to a boil. Cover and
simmer for 10 minutes, or until
berries are cooked down to juice.
Strain the juice into a saucepan and
discard the pulp. Season the juice
with sugar. Mix the potato starch
and 1/4 cup water to form a smooth
paste and pour slowly, mixing well,
into the juice. Place back on heat
and simmer until sauce thickens and
becomes transparent. Stir sauce into
whole strawberries reserved in the
bowl. Chill and serve plain or with
whipped cream.

Chocolate Cake
Soklatkake

*"This is named in 'Finnglish.' I have
been served many pieces of* soklatkake
*throughout my life from wonderful,
grandmotherly Finnish ladies."*
—Beatrice Ojakangas

**3/4 cup butter
1-1/2 cups sugar
3 eggs
1 teaspoon vanilla
2 cups all-purpose flour
3/4 cup unsweetened regular
     dark cocoa
1 teaspoon baking soda
1/2 teaspoon baking powder
1/2 teaspoon salt
1-1/3 cups water
Whipped cream for topping**

In large mixing bowl, cream butter
and sugar until smooth. Add eggs
and beat until light and fluffy. Beat
in the vanilla. In small bowl,
combine flour, cocoa, baking soda,
baking powder, and salt. Add flour
mixture to creamed mixture alternately with the water; beat at high
speed until very light. Preheat oven
to 350°F. Grease a 13 x 9-inch cake
pan. Turn mixture into pan. Bake
45 minutes until cake shrinks away
from edges of pan. Cool. Cut into
squares; top with whipped cream.
Makes 12 servings.

Almond Pound Cake
Mantelikakku

The formal Finnish coffee table always includes an un-iced pound cake as part of the "second course."

3 eggs, separated
1/2 cup butter
1 cup sugar
1 teaspoon almond extract
1/2 cup milk
1-1/3 cups all-purpose flour
1-1/2 teaspoons baking powder
Sliced or slivered almonds
Powdered sugar

Beat egg whites until stiff. Set aside. Cream butter, sugar, egg yolks, and almond extract. Gradually add the milk and beat until light. Combine flour and baking powder. Stir into creamed mixture. Fold in egg whites until just blended. Generously butter a fancy tube-type pan, about 6-cup size. Sprinkle with the sliced or slivered almonds. Turn batter into the pan. Bake at 350°F for 30 to 35 minutes or until the cake tests done. Invert onto cooling rack. Dust with powdered sugar. Makes 8 to 10 servings.

Fancy Filled Cake
Täytekakku

The fancy filled cake is always the principal dish of the Finnish coffee table and is served last. It is generally made of layers of light sponge cake (or buttery pastry), filled with whipped cream and berries. A fruit-flavored liqueur often is soaked into the sponge cake layers.

Cake layers:
4 eggs
1 cup sugar
1 teaspoon vanilla
1 cup all-purpose flour
1/4 teaspoon salt
1/2 teaspoon baking powder

Moistening mixture:
1/2 cup fruit-flavored liqueur
    or orange or apple juice

Filling:
2 cups fresh berries or fruit
2 cups heavy cream, whipped
    stiff, slightly sweetened

Beat eggs, sugar, and vanilla until thick and creamy. Combine flour, salt, and baking powder; stir into egg mixture until blended. Pour

Stealthy skis!
Stealth on skis has often been attributed to the success of Finnish soldiers in conflict. A thirteenth-century publication says, "Now they are close by and soon again they are far away. As soon as they have inflicted damage on the enemy, they rush away as swiftly as they came."
—From Saxo Grammaticus: Gesta Danorum

into two buttered and floured 8- or 9-inch round cake pans. Bake at 375°F for 20 to 25 minutes or until cakes spring back when touched in the center. Remove from oven, cool 10 minutes, and turn out onto wire racks to cool. Split each layer in half horizontally. Sprinkle each layer with liqueur or juice and spread with 1/2 cup fruit and 1/3 cup whipped cream as you stack the layers (there should be 1/2 cup fruit for the top and about half the whipped cream for the edge of the top and the sides of the cake). Chill several hours. Makes 10 to 12 servings.

Easter Cheesecake
Pasha

This delicious cheesy mixture is classically turned into a special pasha *mold, which has Easter symbols embossed on it. Definitely an eastern influence, this Karelian specialty has become popular in Finland in recent years.*

4 quarts buttermilk
1/2 cup (1 stick) butter
1 egg
1 cup sour cream
1/2 cup sugar
1/2 cup finely ground almonds
1/2 teaspoon vanilla extract
Candied fruits
Orange peel
Whipped cream

Put buttermilk into a large pot or casserole. Bake at 250°F for 3 hours. Cool. Turn into a large sieve or strainer lined with cheesecloth. Let drain overnight. Melt butter in a heavy saucepan or in double boiler. Beat egg. Blend egg with the curd from the buttermilk; in the food processor with steel blade, this is easily done. Blend in the sour cream, sugar, almonds, and vanilla. Add the butter, blending well. Place over medium heat and heat the mixture slowly, stirring all the time with a flat-bottomed wooden spoon or with a spatula, being sure not to burn the bottom. Heat to between 190°F and 200°F.

Line a deep wooden *pasha* mold or a 1-quart-sized clean clay pot with a double thickness of cheesecloth. Pour the mixture into the cheesecloth-lined container, lap edges over the top, and place into a bowl. Press down the *pasha* and put a weight on top. Refrigerate for 2 to 3 days. Excess liquid will drop into the bowl. To serve, unmold *pasha* onto a plate. Decorate with candied or fresh fruit and whipped cream. Slice crosswise starting from the top for each serving. Ordinarily this is served just plain. However, a sauce made of cloudberry preserves, heated and thinned with a little water, makes a nice accompaniment. Serves 8 to 10.

Blueberry Cheese Torte

Mustikkarahkatorttu

This is a wonderful cheesecake-like dessert to serve in the summertime when blueberries are fresh. Frozen blueberries or jam work well, too.

Crust:
2 cups all-purpose flour
1 teaspoon baking powder
2 tablespoons sugar
1/2 cup butter
1 egg

Filling:
1 cup creamed small curd
    cottage cheese
1 tablespoon lemon juice
2 teaspoons grated lemon peel
2 teaspoons vanilla
1/2 cup sugar
1/2 cup soft butter
2 eggs, slightly beaten

Topping:
Fresh blueberries, frozen
    unsugared blueberries,
    or blueberry jam
1 cup heavy cream, whipped
    (optional)

To make the crust, sift the flour together with the baking powder and sugar into a mixing bowl. Using a fork, cut in the butter until the mixture resembles coarse crumbs. Beat the egg and pour over the crumb mixture. With fingers, mix ingredients until a dough is formed. Butter a 9-inch removable-bottom tart pan. Pat the mixture into the bottom and sides of the pan.

To prepare filling, whip the cottage cheese until creamy, using an electric mixer. Add the lemon juice, lemon peel, vanilla, sugar, butter, and eggs. Beat until mixture is smooth. Pour into the dough-lined cake pan. Bake at 350°F for 40 to 45 minutes or until filling is set. Cool. Top with the berries or jam. Serve with whipped cream if desired. Makes 8 servings.

Scandinavian Dessert Cake

Jälkiruokakakku

Soile Anderson is noted for her Scandinavian treats.

Cake:
8 eggs
2 cups sugar
1 cup cornstarch
1 cup flour
1 tablespoon baking powder

Filling:
Whipped cream
Bananas, sliced
Strawberry jam
Strawberries or kiwi fruit

Beat eggs; mix with sugar. Add cornstarch, flour, and baking powder.

Bake in large sheet pan (or divide to small pans) at 400°F for 15 minutes.

Slice cake into three layers. Combine whipped cream, bananas, and strawberry jam. Spread mixture between layers. Frost cake with whipped cream and garnish with fresh strawberries or kiwi fruit.

Cardamom Cream Pound Cake
Kardemummakakku

On the coffee table, this often is the un-iced cake, baked in a fancy tube-type mold.

1 cup chilled whipping cream
2 eggs
1 teaspoon vanilla
1 teaspoon freshly ground
   cardamom
1-1/2 cups all-purpose flour
1 cup sugar
2 teaspoons baking powder
1/2 teaspoon salt

In large bowl, whip cream until stiff. Beat eggs and vanilla until light and fluffy and fold in the whipped cream. Fold in remaining ingredients. Pour batter into a greased 9-cup tube-type cake pan. Bake at 350°F until cake pulls away from sides of the pan, 50 to 60 minutes. Cool in pan 10 minutes. Invert onto wire rack; cool completely. Sprinkle with powdered sugar to decorate if desired. Makes 12 servings.

Blueberry Bars
Mustikkapiirakat

The wild blueberry grows in Finland, Canada, and in the northern United States. These butter-crusted bars are cut into small pieces, or if for dessert, cut into large squares.

Crust:
2-1/2 cups all-purpose flour
1/2 cup sugar
1 egg, lightly beaten
1/2 teaspoon baking powder
1 cup soft butter

Filling:
2 cups blueberries
4 tablespoons sugar
1 tablespoon lemon juice
1 tablespoon grated lemon rind
2 tablespoons cornstarch
1/4 teaspoon salt

To make the crust, blend the flour, sugar, egg, and baking powder in a large mixing bowl. Blend in the butter until mixture resembles fine crumbs. With hands, press these together into a dough. Roll dough out on a lightly floured board to fit a 10 x 15-inch jelly roll pan, reserving about 1/2 cup of the dough to use on top. The dough is a bit crumbly, but you can pick it up in pieces and "patch" it together into the pan. With fingers, form a ridge around the edge of the dough so the filling will not run over during the baking.

Prepare filling: pour blueberries

into a small mixing bowl. Stir in the sugar, lemon juice, lemon rind, cornstarch, and salt. Spread the filling over the dough in the pan.

Roll out the reserved portion of dough on floured board to 1/8-inch thickness. Cut into strips and place in a criss-cross pattern over the filling. Sprinkle the top with additional sugar, if desired. Bake at 375°F for 25 to 30 minutes or until crust is golden. Cut into squares to serve. Makes 12 desserts; 48 bars.

Pinwheel Prune Tarts with Yeast Pastry
Luumutortut

Ruth Park Johnson
Makinen, Minnesota

Pastry:
1 cup all-purpose flour
1 small package compressed yeast
4 cups all-purpose flour
2 cups margarine
4 egg yolks
1 cup commercial sour cream

Filling:
1/2 pound prunes
1 cup water
1/8 teaspoon cream of tartar
1/2 cup sugar (or to taste)
Powdered sugar

In a large bowl, rub the 1 cup flour with the yeast with hands until mixture resembles fine crumbs. Add the 4 cups flour and cut in the margarine until the mixture resembles coarse crumbs. Blend egg yolks and sour cream. Add egg mixture to the crumbly mixture, tossing until blended. Refrigerate overnight.

To prepare filling, cook prunes in water until prunes are tender. Cool. Remove pits and return prunes to juice. Add cream of tartar and sugar. Cook until thick. Mash with fork into coarse purée. Cool.

Roll out portions of dough thinner than for pie crust. Cut into 3-inch squares using a sharp knife. Cut into corners, as for making pinwheels, leaving intact a small section in the center for the filling. Place a scant teaspoon of filling onto center of each pastry square. Turn to center every other corner; overlap slightly in the center and moisten corner tips lightly. Press a bit with tip of paring knife to seal. Bake on cookie sheet at 375°F 10 to 15 minutes until very light brown. Sprinkle with sifted powdered sugar to serve. Leftovers are good if warmed slightly before serving. I usually make up only a portion of these at a time so as to have them "freshly made." Pastry and filling will keep refrigerated for several weeks.

Christmas Prune Tarts
Joulutortut

Mrs. Dorothy Tamminen
Pengilly, Minnesota
These Finnish tarts are always a part
of her Christmas baking.

Pastry:
4 cups all-purpose flour
1 pound butter, divided
3/4 cup cold water

Filling:
1 pound pitted, stewed prunes
1/2 cup sugar

To prepare pastry, cut flour and 1/2 pound of butter until mixture resembles coarse crumbs. Add the water. Chill 30 minutes. Roll out and dot with 1/4 pound butter. Fold dough from front toward back, from back to front, and from each side toward center. Chill. Repeat process of rolling and chilling, adding dots of butter, 3 times or until all butter is used. Roll again. Cut into 3-inch squares. Slit each corner of each square.

Mix stewed prunes and sugar. Place a spoonful of prune filling in the center of each square. Turn up alternating corners (as in making a pinwheel) and pinch together in the center. Chill. Bake in 400°F oven for 13 to 15 minutes until golden. Cool on brown paper.

Cranberry Parfait
Karpalojäädyke

Mrs. Helena Iloniemi, Finland

8 egg yolks
3/4 cup sugar
3/4 cup cranberry-apple juice
 or water
4 cups cranberries
1-1/2 cups sugar (additional)
Water
3 cups whipped cream

For decoration:
1 cup whole cranberries
1 cup water
1 cup sugar
Powdered sugar

Beat egg yolks, 3/4 cup sugar, and juice in the top of a double boiler over high heat. Stir constantly until it thickens. Cool.

Put cranberries into a saucepan and add the 1-1/2 cups sugar and water to cover. Cook until cranberries pop; purée. Cool.

Pour mixture of egg yolks, sugar, and juice into the whipped cream and stir until blended. Pour into cranberry purée. Stir well. Before pouring mixture into parfait glasses, wet the parfait glasses with cold water. Freeze.

For the decoration: Boil cranberries in 1 cup each of water and sugar for 5 minutes. Strain out cranberries; cool and coat with powdered sugar. Use to garnish the tray.

−151

Christmas Piggy Cookies
Nissu Nassu

Children in Finland know that Christmas is coming when they begin to see these piggy-shaped cookies in the bakeries! Crispy and spicy, the cookies are made of piparkakku *dough as is this one. However, this dough retains its shape beautifully, without spreading much as it bakes.* Nissu nassu *are children's pet names for pigs. You may pipe a name across the back of each cookie just as it is done in Finnish bakeries.*

3/4 cup softened butter
3/4 cup brown sugar
1 tablespoon cinnamon
2 teaspoons ground ginger
1 teaspoon ground cloves
1-1/2 teaspoons baking soda
2-1/2 cups all-purpose flour
1/4 cup water

Cream the butter and sugar together until blended. Mix the cinnamon, ginger, cloves, soda, and flour. Add to the butter-sugar mixture. Blend well. Stir in the water until dough is smooth and pliable (depending on conditions, you may need to add a teaspoon more water to the dough). Chill if necessary before rolling out. Roll out and cut into pig shapes with a pig-shaped cookie cutter. Place on lightly greased cookie sheets and bake at 375°F for 7 to 10 minutes until very lightly browned and crisp. Decorate, if desired, with frosting made of powdered sugar and egg white. Makes 5 to 6 dozen cookies.

Note: In Finland, this recipe is known as *Nisset ja Nasset*.

Finnish "S" Cookies
Ässät

Buttery little S-shaped cookies are perfect on the holiday cookie tray.

1/2 cup softened butter
1/4 cup sugar
1 egg
1/2 teaspoon almond extract
Dash of salt
1-1/2 to 1-3/4 cups all-purpose
    flour
1 egg, beaten
Sugar
1/4 cup finely chopped toasted
    almonds

In large mixing bowl, cream butter, 1/4 cup sugar, 1 egg, the almond extract, and salt until light and fluffy. Stir in enough flour to make dough easy to handle. Blend with hands until smooth. Shape dough into long strands, 1/2 inch thick. Cut into 2-1/2-inch lengths. Dip into beaten egg; roll in sugar, then in almonds. Arrange "S" shapes on greased baking sheets. Bake at 375°F until golden, about 8 minutes. Cool on wire racks. Makes 3-1/2 dozen.

Teaspoon Cookies
Lusikkaleivät

Marlene Banttari, St. Paul
From The Finnish Cookbook *by*
Beatrice A. Ojakangas

1 cup butter
3/4 cup sugar
3 teaspoons vanilla
2 cups all-purpose flour
1 teaspoon baking soda
Strawberry jam

Brown the butter to a pale tan color in a small heavy saucepan. Cool. Pour into mixing bowl. Stir in sugar and vanilla. Combine flour and soda; add gradually to butter mixture. Stir until mixture is uniformly crumbly.

To shape a cookie, press dough firmly into a teaspoon, leveling top. Tap side of spoon on cookie sheet to gently remove cookie. Bake at 325°F for 6 to 8 minutes until barely brown. Remove carefully onto foil to cool.

Spread jam on the flat side of one cookie. Press second cookie to form almond-shaped sandwich cookie. Cookies can be frozen to store. Flavor improves with time. Makes 4 dozen.

Spicy Ginger Cookies
Piparkakut

This is a popular cookie all year long. Most of the year the cookies are cut into a scalloped round shape. At Christmastime, Finnish bakers make hearts, pigs, gingerbread ladies and men, and other shapes, decorating them with icing.

1/2 cup soft butter
3/4 cup sugar
1 egg
2 teaspoons dark corn syrup
1-1/2 cups all-purpose flour
1 teaspoon baking soda
1-1/2 teaspoons ground
** ginger**
1 teaspoon cinnamon
1/4 teaspoon cloves

Cream the butter, sugar, egg, and corn syrup until light and fluffy. Stir in the remaining ingredients until blended. Chill 1 hour. Roll 1/16 inch thick on lightly floured surface. Cut into shapes with cookie cutters; place 1 inch apart on lightly greased baking sheets; bake at 375°F for 6 to 8 minutes or until just barely browned. Makes about 5 dozen.

Rye Cookies
Ruiskakut

These thin little cookie rounds mimic the look of Finnish rye breads with a hole in the center and holes poked into the surface of the cookie.

1/2 cup (1 stick) softened butter
1/3 cup sugar
1 to 1-1/2 cups rye flour
1/2 cup all-purpose flour
1 egg, slightly beaten
Sugar

In a bowl, cream butter and sugar until light. Stir in rye flour and all-purpose flour; mix in the egg and work dough with hands until smooth. Roll on lightly floured board to 1/8-inch thickness. Cut into 2-inch rounds. Sprinkle with sugar.

Place cookies 1 inch apart on lightly greased baking sheets. Cut a little 1/2-inch hole just off center of each cookie. Prick entire surface with a fork. Bake at 375°F for 5 to 7 minutes until lightly browned. Makes 3-1/2 dozen.

Spritz Butter Cookies
Voivannikkeet

Buttery and tender, these cookies are especially good Christmastime treats.

2 cups butter
2 cups sugar
1 egg
1 teaspoon vanilla
1 teaspoon almond extract
1/4 teaspoon salt
1 teaspoon baking powder
4 cups all-purpose flour

Cream butter, sugar, egg, vanilla, and almond extract until fluffy. Stir in salt, baking powder, and flour just until blended. Chill 30 minutes. Put dough into cookie press fitted with the star disk. Press out onto cookie sheets making straight 2-inch lengths and "S" shapes. Bake at 375°F until just set, not browned, about 8 minutes. Makes about 10 dozen.

Finns have traditionally consumed a great deal of whole-grain breads including rye. The beneficial effects of the fiber, minerals, and vitamins attributed to rye are of continuing scientific interest. The Finnish bakery industry is making an effort to export its rye products.

Loaves of cracked wheat bread cooling for a Laskiainen *festival in northern Minnesota*

May Day Crullers

Tippaleivät

This is a thin yeast batter which is drizzled into hot fat to make somewhat of a "bird's nest" shape, then fried as you would a doughnut. Delicious, tippaleivät are traditionally served on May 1, the big springtime student holiday in Finland.

4 eggs
1 tablespoon sugar
2 cups milk (105°– 115°F)
1 package active dry yeast
4 cups all-purpose flour
Hot fat for frying
Powdered sugar

Beat eggs and sugar together. Blend in the milk and yeast; stir until yeast is dissolved. Add flour, beating to keep mixture smooth. Cover and let mixture rise until bubbly, about 1 hour. Place batter into a pastry bag or a plastic container with a 1/4-inch nozzle tip in the end. Heat fat to 375°F and drizzle batter into the fat, making round swirls and a bird's nest shape. Fry until golden on one side, turn over and cook until golden, then remove and drain on paper toweling. Dust with powdered sugar and serve hot. Makes about 4 dozen.

Welcome!
Snow lanterns are unique to the north countries. Firmly packed snowballs are used to build a pyramid shape with a tiny candle placed inside, creating a flickering welcome beacon.

Dessert Pancakes

Ohukaiset

Tyyne Lothberg, Virginia, Minnesota Originally from Merikarvia, Finland, Tyyne came to the United States in 1955 and has been an active member of the Ladies of Kaleva of Virginia for many years. She was a cook at Salolampi, the Concordia College Finnish Language Camp at Bemidji, Minnesota, for 12 years. Along with other sisters of Kaleva, she has taught Finnish cooking and food presentation.

3 eggs
2 cups milk
1 tablespoon sugar
1 teaspoon salt
3/4 cup flour
Butter

Beat eggs lightly. Add milk. Mix in sugar, salt, and flour. Let set for a minimum of 1/2 hour. Heat an 8-inch omelet pan. When hot add about 1/2 teaspoon butter and swirl around the pan. Add two tablespoons of batter and swirl around pan to distribute. When the pancake is brown and lacey, turn and brown the other side. Remove from pan and roll up. These can be reheated. If they are to be filled with fruit such as berries, they can be rolled after they cool. Top with a dab of whipped cream. Delicious!

Finnish Oven Pancake #1

Pannukakku

Gerry Kangas, Aurora, Minnesota
Pannukakku *is an oven pancake that is sometimes called* kropsu. *Originally made from "new milk" or colostrum diluted with whole milk, it didn't puff up like these, but was richer. Gerry says she prefers to add the evaporated milk for the richer taste. Her grandparents sprinkled sugar on cold pancakes and rolled them up for a snack. Gerry serves them hot with berry jam or maple syrup.*

1/4 cup butter
2 eggs
2 cups whole milk or 1 cup
  whole milk and 1 cup
  evaporated milk
1 cup all-purpose flour
2 tablespoons sugar
1 teaspoon salt

Preheat oven to 375°F. Melt butter in two 8-inch round pans in hot oven. Teflon or Baker's Secret pans are excellent. A 13 x 9-inch pan can be used, but the two round pans are preferred. In a large bowl, beat eggs with a wire whisk and add milk, flour, sugar, and salt, beating until mixture is very smooth. Pour batter into the sizzling hot pans and bake for 30 to 40 minutes. Remove from pans as soon as possible to avoid sticking. Makes 8 servings.

156–

Finnish Oven Pancake #2

Pannukakku

Mrs. Helena Iloniemi, Finland
This is another version of pannukakku *or* kropsu. *As is typical of authentic, basic foods, every cook has his or her own favorite ingredient proportions. Mrs. Iloniemi serves this with strawberry preserves.*

4 eggs
2 tablespoons sugar
2-1/2 to 3 cups milk
1 teaspoon salt
1-1/2 to 2 cups unbleached
  all-purpose flour

Preheat oven to 425°F. In a large bowl, beat eggs and sugar until thick and foamy. Add milk and salt. Stir in half the flour and beat well. The batter should have a firm structure so it can rise in the oven. Stir in the other half of the flour and keep beating for about 10 minutes.

Grease a 3-inch-deep oven pan. Pour the batter into the pan and put into the oven immediately. Bake 20 to 25 minutes. The pancake will bubble and parts of it will rise; the top and sides should be brown, the insides still a little chewy. Makes 4 to 6 servings.

Note: *Pannukakku* can be frozen and reheated. Use a microwave oven to reheat.

Finnish Oven Pancake #3

Pannukakku

Mal Rowe, Marquette, Michigan
This pannukakku *or* kropsu *has a higher proportion of milk and flour to egg, compared to the other two versions in this collection.*

4 cups (1 quart) milk
4 to 5 eggs
1/2 teaspoon salt
1/4 to 1/2 cup sugar, as desired
4 to 5 cups all-purpose flour
Butter

Preheat oven to 450°F. In a large bowl, beat together the milk, eggs, salt, and sugar. Add the flour and blend. Batter should be rather thin. Generously butter two 8- or 9-inch round pans or one 9 x 13-inch pan. Put enough batter just to cover the bottom of the pan. Bake on lowest rack of oven until brown around the edges, about 10 minutes. Then lift pans to top rack and bake until bubbly and delicately brown, another 10 minutes. Remove from oven and

Chain saw sculpture of St. Urho Finland, Minnesota

loosen edges with a table knife or spatula. Top with additional butter if desired; may also be topped with syrup or sprinkled with sugar. This is best when piping hot. Simply delicious! Yields about 10 8-inch pancakes.

Menus

St. Urho's Day Celebration March 16, Dinner

Kalamojakka (Fish Stew)
Pyhän Urhon ruisleipä
(St. Urho's Rye Bread)
Hardtack (bakery made)
Butter
Vegetable Sticks
Soklatkake (Chocolate Cake)

May Day Open House
Sima
Tippaleivät

Christmas Eve Menu

Christmas Ham with Prunes
Mashed Potato Casserole
Carrot Casserole
Rutabaga Casserole
Cucumber Salad
Beet Salad
Finnish Christmas Rye Bread
Creamy Oven Rice Pudding
Fruit Soup

Coffee Table Menu

Finnish Cardamom Coffee
Bread *(Pulla)*
Almond Pound Cake
Fancy Filled Cake
Spicy Ginger Cookies
Blueberry Bars
Spritz Butter Cookies
Rye Cookies

Menu For Casual Entertaining
Fish Pie
Old-Fashioned Salad
Cranberry Parfait

Metric Conversion Table

Volume Measures

American (Standard Cup)		Metric
1 cup	= 1/2 pint	2.37 dl.
	= 8 fl. oz.	
1 Tbs.	= 1/2 fl. oz.	1.5 cl.
1 tsp.	= 1/6 fl. oz.	0.5 cl.
1 pint	= 16 fl. oz.	4.73 dl.
1 quart	= 2 pints	9.46 dl.
	= 32 fl. oz.	

Weight Measures

American		Metric
1 lb.	= 16 oz.	453 grams
2.2 lbs.		1000 grams = 1 kilogram
1 oz.		28 grams
3-1/2 oz.		100 grams

Oven Temperature

Fahrenheit	Celsius
275°F	135°C
325°F	160°C
350°F	175°C
375°F	190°C
400°F	205°C
450°F	230°C

Books by Mail

$14.95 *Finnish Touches: Recipes and Traditions Fantastically Finnish Revised & Expanded*
$10.95 *Finnish Proverbs* translated by Inkeri Väänänen-Jensen
$ 6.95 *Fine Finnish Foods* compiled by Gerry Kangas
       (160 page recipe-card-file size, spiral bound) (this book only $9.95 postpaid)
$12.95 *Finnfun* by Bernhard Hillila
$12.95 *The F!nn!sh L!ne: More F!nnfun* by Bernhard H!ll!ha
$12.95 *Suomi Specialties: Finnish Celebrations* by Sinikka Grönberg Garcia
$12.95 *Words of Wisdom and Magic from the Kalevala,* translated by
       Richard Impola (See verse from this book on page 160)
$17.95 *Finnish Short Stories* Revised & Expanded
$ 2.00 Complete catalog including all Finnish titles available
Prices subject to change.
(Shipping: $4.95; for orders over $25.00 add $5.95.)
Please send personal check.
Credit card orders call: 1-800-728-9998.

Penfield Books
215 Brown Street
Iowa City, Iowa 52245

Lönnrot's *valedictory*

Time for me to cease my singing,
tie my tongue up in a knot....
I'll wind my verse up in a ball...
stow it in the storehouse loft....
Many have complained to me,
cursed my verse or damned my accent...

But still in all, at any rate,
I have broken trail for others,
set the course and cleared the way
for better, more prolific singers,
for the younger folk,
for the rising generation.

50: 611-620

From Words of Wisdom and Magic from the
Kalevala *translated by Richard Impola*

CPSIA information can be obtained
at www.ICGtesting.com
Printed in the USA
BVHW041531301121
622873BV000011B/660

9 781737 839903